Achieve
IELTS

English for International Education

Student's Book

Louis Harrison
Caroline Cushen

Marshall Cavendish
Education

About *Achieve IELTS*

Achieve IELTS is a new course designed to prepare students for success in the International English Language Testing System. *Achieve IELTS* takes students from band 4.5 (limited user) to band 6 (competent user) – the IELTS score many Universities require for international students on undergraduate courses.

Achieve IELTS features questions, tasks and instructions that closely follow the questions, tasks and instructions in the test to make sure students are well-prepared in advance for the test. The course also prepares students for academic life after IELTS by giving them the language and cross-cultural knowledge to deal with life in international education.

Author team

Louis Harrison teaches at the University of Bradford on IELTS preparation courses as well as pre-sessional and foundation courses. He has taught in the UK, Turkey, Hungary and Sri Lanka and is an experienced author having written several English Language teaching books

Caroline Cushen is a current IELTS examiner with five years' testing experience overseas and in the UK. She has taught in Spain, Hungary, Indonesia, Malaysia and Vietnam. She is currently teaching on EAP Foundation and MA TESOL Programmes at the University of Buckingham.

Susan Hutchison is a teacher trainer and examiner who worked for many years with the British Council where she was involved in the development of the British Council IELTS CD-Rom project. She has taught in the UK, Italy, Hungary and currently teaches English at The British International School in Moscow.

The authors would like to give special thanks to Simon Ross of Marshall Cavendish ELT; Philip Saltmarsh of Eötvös Loránd University, Budapest; Andrea Liptak; Györgyi Gyetvai (Unit 12, Writing); Irona Dougherty and Stefan Ridley (the University of Buckingham) and Dr Joan Rees (Unit 9); William Skyrme, the British Council, Moscow, Ahmed Hossini; Graham Harding, the University of Bradford.

Most of all we would like to thank students at the University of Bradford, the University of Buckingham and at the British Council, Moscow who worked through Achieve IELTS and gave us invaluable feedback and suggestions.

For Laurie and Sylvia, Ted, and Eva.

Contents

Unit	Title	Page
	Introduction	2
1	On course	4
2	Campus	15
3	Living space	25
4	Film society	36
5	Bulletin	47
6	Energy	57
7	Cities	70
8	Communication	79
9	Fitness and health	89
10	Charities	99
11	Work	109
12	Academic success	119
	Assignments	130
	Audioscripts	136

Map of the book

Unit/title	Page	Test practice	
Introduction	2	test overview / *Achieve IELTS* survey	
1 On course	4	Speaking	introduction
		Reading	matching headings and paragraphs; multiple-choice questions
		Listening	table completion; note completion
		Writing	task 1 – introducing a report
2 Campus	15	Reading	matching headings and paragraphs; classification
		Speaking	individual long turn – introducing a topic; rounding-off questions (1)
		Listening	labelling; short answers
		Writing	task 1 – describing change
3 Living space	25	Listening	multiple-choice questions; sentence completion
		Reading	yes/no/not given; multiple-choice questions; summarising
		Speaking	individual long turn – giving personal information
		Writing	task 1 – task achievement
4 Film society	36	Reading	true/false/not given; multiple-choice questions
		Listening	table completion; short answers
		Speaking	individual long turn – giving longer answers (1)
		Writing	task 1 – referring to numbers
5 Bulletin	47	Listening	note completion; table completion
		Reading	multiple-choice questions
		Speaking	individual long turn – giving longer answers (2)
		Writing	task 1 – giving reasons
6 Energy	57	Reading	true/false/not given; labelling a diagram
		Writing	describing a process
		Listening	labelling a diagram
		Speaking	individual long turn; rounding-off questions (2)
7 Cities	70	Speaking	individual long turn – describing cities
		Reading	matching headings and paragraphs, table completion; true/false/not given
		Listening	labelling; note completion; table completion
		Writing	task 1 – comparing and contrasting changes
8 Communication	79	Reading	labelling, classification
		Speaking	individual long turn – descriptions (1); discussion
		Listening	note completion
		Writing	discursive essay – preparation
9 Fitness and health	89	Listening	note completion; matching
		Reading	yes/no/not given; summarising
		Speaking	individual long turn – descriptions (2); discussion
		Writing	discursive essay – topic sentences
10 Charities	99	Reading	yes/no/not given; summarising
		Speaking	individual long turn – definitions and examples; discussion
		Listening	note completion; table completion; multiple-choice questions
		Writing	discursive essay – introductions and conclusions
11 Work	109	Reading	multiple-choice questions; true/false/not given
		Listening	table completion; note completion
		Writing	discursive essay – examples and definitions
		Speaking	introduction; individual long turn; discussion – giving opinions
12 Academic success	119	Listening	note completion; multiple-choice questions
		Writing	discursive essay – proofreading
		Reading	matching headings and paragraphs; true/false/not given; summarising
		Speaking	introduction; individual long turn; discussion - rephrasing
Assignments	130		
Audioscripts	136		

Language study	Pronunciation	*Achieve IELTS*	Expressions
present continuous present simple	number, dates and addresses	words with similar and contrasting meanings referring to titles	asking for and giving spellings talking about things in common
giving directions general amounts	asking for directions	repeated information	asking for repetition
will / going to *must (n't), need to / have to*	final *-y*	talking about your home task achievement	talking about untidiness
narrative tenses suggestions	suggestions	giving longer answers	talking about films
present perfect giving reasons		reading for general understanding	personal information
information questions present passive sequence and purpose		predicting	free time
comparatives superlatives	rise / fall intonation	comparing graphs	talking about cities
real conditionals *unless, in case*	sentence stress	cue words timing and length	disbelief
should (n't), must (n't) possibility and certainty	*should (n't)*	descriptions	talking about ability
giving more information (defining and non-defining relative clauses)	linking	giving definitions and examples	asking for details
preference second conditional opinions	intonation	giving examples	saying goodbye
gerunds	/ŋ/	assessing your essay	apologies and excuses rephrasing

Introduction

Test overview, *Achieve IELTS* survey

1   Do the quiz.

IELTS quiz

How much do you know about IELTS? Try this quiz and find out. Circle the answers that you think are correct.

❶ IELTS means …

A   International English Language Testing System.   ▪

B   International English Language Testing Standard.   ▪

❷ There are two modules …

A   the academic and general training modules.   ▪

B   the academic and English language modules.   ▪

❸ The academic module is for students who would like to …

A   study at a university or college.   ▪

B   study at a training school.   ▪

❹ IELTS has _____ parts.

A 3   ▪   B 4   ▪   C 2   ▪

❺ IELTS takes …

A   I hour 35 minutes.   ▪

B   2 hours 14 minutes.   ▪

C   2 hours 44 minutes.   ▪

   Now listen and check your answers.

 2   Listen again and complete the chart.

part	time	sections/tasks/text	questions
I *listening*			*10 questions*
2	*one hour*		
3		*two tasks*	—
4			—

3   Look through *Achieve IELTS* and answer the questions.

1   How many sections does each unit of *Achieve IELTS* have? What are they?

2   Where can you find vocabulary for IELTS?

3   Where can you find advice on how to do well in the test?

4   How many language points are covered in *Achieve IELTS*?

4   **Work in pairs. Discuss the questions.**

1   Which part of the test do you think you are good at?

2   Which part of the test do you think you need to practise?

3   Which part of the test do you think you will enjoy?

5   **Match the words in A with the definitions.**

1   an activity in which students put information into groups

2   a type of question for which students choose the answer from a number of possible answers

3   an activity in which students read or listen and write the name of something next to its picture

4   an activity in which students read and write the main points

5   an activity in which students read and choose the best title for a paragraph

A

multiple-choice questions
choosing headings
labelling
classification
summarising

Now work in pairs. Decide which questions or activities are in the listening test and which are in the reading test.

6   **Work in pairs. Complete the table with one example of each question type in *Achieve IELTS*.**

Achieve IELTS survey	listening	reading	writing	speaking
multiple choice	(1) *Unit 1, Listening, activity 3*	(5)	(13) task 1	(15) introduction
short answer questions	(2)	(6)	(14) task 2	(16) individual long turn *Unit 4, speaking activity 2*
chart/table/note/ sentence completion	(3)	(7)		(17) discussion
labelling	(4)	(8)		
choosing headings		(9)		
yes, no, not given		(10)		
true, false, not given		(11)		
summarising		(12)		

Now work in pairs and ask each other the questions.

1   Which topics in *Achieve IELTS* are you interested in?

2   Which question types do think you need to practise?

UNIT 1
On course

Registration day

1 Look at the picture above and say what is happening.

Now match the words in A with their definitions.

1 this person organises the courses and does the office work
2 to become a student on a course
3 this person decides which students can go to a university or college
4 to put your name on an official list
5 the name of a course at a university or college

2 Read the card and answer the questions.

Registration day: School of Management

Enrolment time	Surname	Place
9 am to 10.30 am	A–H	Great Hall, E floor
11 am to 12.30 pm	I–O	Great Hall, E floor
1 pm to 2.30 pm	P–Z	Small Hall, E floor
2 pm to 4 pm	Timetable collection from course administrator	

Welcome packs are available on registration. Students who would like to change course should see the admissions officer in F11 before enrolment.

1 What time does Belen Pérez register?
2 Where does Belen Pérez register?
3 When are Welcome packs available?

3   Read the registration form. Write a question for each section.

Registration form: International Business and Management Studies

Last name(s)	(1) _Pérez_	Tel number(s)	(5) _____
First name(s)	(2) _Belen_	Date of birth	(6) _____
School	(3) _____	Marital status	(7) _____
Course code	(4) _____	E-mail	(8) _____

 Now listen to a conversation and complete the form for Belen.

 4   Listen again and answer the questions.

1 Why is it important to get Belen's name right?
2 What's wrong with Belen's phone?
3 What does she do after registration?

Express yourself: asking for and giving spellings

We can use these phrases to spell and check spellings.

Could you repeat that please?   *No, just one L.*
Could you say that again?   *That's right/correct.*
That's R for river.   *I think I've got that now.*
Is that with double L?

 Now listen and practise.

---

5   Work in pairs. Ask each other questions and complete the registration form.

6   Work in pairs. Decide what you can talk about when you first meet another student.

1 the course you are taking
2 your timetable
3 your accommodation
4 how much you paid for the course
5 who your tutor is

 Now listen to a conversation and tick the things they talk about.

7   Label the diagram. Use the words in B.

 Now listen again and answer the questions.
1 Which department is Tao in?
2 Which courses are the students taking?
3 What is Tao trying to decide?
4 What do Tao and Belen want to talk about?

B
faculty
department
school
centre/unit

Language study: present continuous

8   Study the examples and explanations.

> *I'm doing Business and Marketing Studies.*
>
> *to be* + verb *-ing*
>
> **We use the present continuous to talk about a temporary situation that has not finished.**
>
> *I'm still trying to decide …*
>
> **We use *still* to emphasis that the action is continuing.**
>
> *Are you doing the four- or three-year course?*
>
> *to be* + subject + verb *-ing*
>
> *What are you taking?*
>
> *Wh-* question + *to be* + subject + verb *-ing*
>
> *We're probably taking similar subjects.*
> *I'm also taking an undergraduate degree.*
>
> **For courses and subjects we often use *do* or *take*.**
>
> *Are you picking up your timetable now?*
>
> **We often use the present continuous to talk about events in the near future.**

C
do
go
take
do
try
take

Now complete the conversation. Use the words in C.

A: Hi Vicky, what (1) _____ you _____ ?

B: I (2) _____ to the Small Hall to register.

A: What course (3) _____ you _____ ?

B: I (4) _____ Economics and Development Studies.

A: (5) _____ you _____ the three- or four-year course?

B: Don't ask! I (6) _____ still _____ to decide.

Express yourself: talking about things in common

We can use these expressions to talk about things we have in common.

We're both in the same hall.

We're probably taking similar subjects.

I'm also taking an undergraduate degree.

We've certainly got something in common.

Aren't you in the same hall as me?

Yes, me too.

 Now listen and underline the stressed words.

---

9   Go around the class and find a student you have three things in common with.

Speaking

IELTS tasks: introduction

1 **Match the words and phrases with the pictures.**

1 Hiya.   2 Good morning.   3 Let me introduce myself ...

A

2 **Work in pairs. Tick the topics the examiner may ask you about.**

1 your hometown ☐
2 your job ☐
3 your studies ☐
4 your income ☐
5 your family ☐
6 your journey ☐

Now match topics 1–6 with questions A–E.

A What do you do? _____
B What subject(s) are you taking? _____
C Do you come from a large family? _____
D Are you from this area? _____
E How long did it take to get here? _____

B

3 **Decide who says these sentences. Write *examiner* or *candidate*.**

☐	Not too far. About half an hour away.	candidate
1	How are you today?	examiner
☐	Could you spell that for me, please?	_____
☐	My name is Erzsébet.	_____
☐	It's E-R-Z-S-É-B-E-T. But you can call me Liz – it's easier.	_____
☐	Yes, of course. It's 062266.	_____
☐	And your name is ...?	_____
☐	Not so good. The traffic is terrible in the city centre.	_____
☐	How was your journey here?	_____
2	Very well, thank you.	_____
☐	Do you live far away?	_____
☐	Can you tell me your candidate number?	_____

C

Now order the conversation.

6 **4** **Listen and check your answers.**

Pronunciation

7 **5** **Listen and write the numbers, dates and addresses.**

8 **6** **Listen and practise the addresses and numbers.**

7 **Work in pairs. Practise the conversation in 3.**

Reading

IELTS tasks: matching headings and paragraphs; multiple-choice questions

D

fresher
tuition
term
lecture
campus
Chancellor

1 **Match the words in D with the definitions.**

1 the teaching time on a course
2 a student in their first year at university or college
3 a talk, usually at university or college, to teach a large group of students
4 a period of time at a school or university; there are usually three of these
5 the area that contains the main buildings of a university
6 the head of the university

2 **This reading passage has five sections A–E. Choose the most suitable heading for each section from the list.**

List of headings	
i The Union	v Student discounts
ii Meeting the Chancellor	vi The first week – what happens
iii A different way of learning	vii Registering
iv Free time	

1 Section A _____
2 Section B _____
3 Section C _____
4 Section D _____
5 Section E _____

A GUARANTEED GOOD TIME

A Many people think life comes with no guarantees. However, freshers' week at university is guaranteed to be the most fun (and the most expensive) week of your life. You meet many new people (a lot of whom you never see again after the first two weeks), find your way around campus, and spend lots of money on tuition and accommodation and, of course, on going out. The purpose of freshers' week is to get all the new students
5 registered on their courses, allow everyone to settle into their accommodation, get timetables sorted out and to receive an introductory talk from the Chancellor of the university. The real reason for most people to attend freshers' week is to have a really good time.

B Unfortunately, you have to go through with the registration and talks, or you may not be listed in course timetables, not receive a union card (essential to student life) and quite possibly have no grant cheque. For
10 registration, find out where and when you are due to register. This information is usually sent to you in the post before you go to the university. The time you register probably depends on which course you are taking, and the initial letter of your surname. Those people with surnames A–H are usually early-morning registration sessions.

C It soon becomes clear at the end of registration that it is all worthwhile, when you are finally given your
15 passport to student life: the Students' Union card. This small credit card-sized ID card gets you into many

nightclubs cheaply, gets you discounts at quite a few shops and fast food chains, and, most importantly, gets you into the Students' Union. The Students' Union is where students spend most of their evenings in freshers' week. Throughout freshers' week, remember this golden rule: enjoy yourself. Do not go to the bookshop and buy all the books on the reading list with the idea of finishing them before lectures start. You do have to work
20 when the term begins, but not during freshers' week.

D The approach to work at university is very different from work at a school or college. You are expected to do a great deal of studying outside lectures, without being asked to do it. Most degree courses have some time set aside for small groups of students to meet a tutor and discuss any questions they have about the lecture, and also to go over problem sheets. It is essential to prepare for these before the classes. Each week, make a note
25 of any problems you have understanding work in lectures, and mention these in your tutorial.

E Try to take advantage of what free time you have to the full. Using your free Wednesday afternoon (set aside by most universities as an afternoon off, for sporting activities) to play your favourite sport is a great way to relax.

3   **Read the passage again and choose four letters a–g.**

During freshers' week new students …
a   move into their rooms.
b   are in the Students' Union for most of the evenings.
c   listen to the Chancellor of the University.
d   read all the books on their reading lists.
e   with first names beginning with C register early in the morning.
f   read and discuss problem sheets.
g   receive Students' Union cards.

Achieve IELTS: words with similar and contrasting meanings

Questions often contain words with similar and contrasting meanings to words in the passage. When you learn a new word try to learn words with similar and contrasting meanings at the same time.

words with similar meanings: *accommodation* ➤ *rooms*

words with contrasting meanings: *talk* ➤ *listen to*

Now find two more examples of a similar word or phrase and a contrasting word or phrase in the reading passage and a–g in 3.

---

4   **Work in pairs. Decide which things are the same in your country.**

Students …
1   get a reading list, then buy and study the books on it.
2   go over problem sheets with the tutor.
3   prepare before class.
4   discuss lectures with the tutor.
5   have tutorials with small groups of students and a tutor.

Now discuss the main differences between …
1   university and school.
2   universities in the UK and your country.

Listening

IELTS tasks: table completion; note completion

1 **Work in pairs. Discuss the questions.**

1 Are you interested in business?

2 What subjects do you think business students study?

2 **Match the words in E with the definitions.**

E
seminar
workshop
tutorial

1 A discussion of a subject where people share their ideas and experience.

2 A regular meeting between a university teacher and a small group of students.

3 A meeting where a group of people discuss a subject from a lecture or a problem.

 3 **Listen to a conversation between a student and a course administrator. Circle T (true) or F (false).**

1 The administrator knows who the student is.   T / F

2 Wednesday is free for sport and other activities.   T / F

3 There are three language courses.   T / F

 Now listen again and complete the timetable.

International Business and Management Studies: term 1 timetable

Monday	Tuesday	Wednesday	Thursday	Friday
am	*am*	*am*	*am*	*am*
10–12	9–10	9–11	9–10	10–11
Languages for Business (French)	Organisational Behaviour, level 1	Foundations of Production Lecture room 2	(4) _____ Systems Lecture room 2	(9) _____ Issues in Business Main lecture theatre
Language laboratory	(1) _____			
	11–12 Tutorial		11–12 Tutorial	
pm	*pm*	*pm*	*pm*	*pm*
	(2) _____ Foundations of Marketing Lecture room 2	12–1 Tutorial	12–1 (5) _____ Study skills	1–2 Languages for Business (10) _____ Language laboratory
		(3) _____ room 3	(6) _____ Foundations of (7) _____ Main lecture theatre (8) _____	

Language study: present simple

4   Study the examples and explanations.

Are you the course administrator?

We use the present simple to talk about something that does not change for a long period – for example where we come from, our job and so on.

You have lectures every morning.

We use the present simple to talk about things that happen regularly. We can say how often it happens with words like *every*, *often*, *sometimes*, *always* and *never*.

On Tuesday you start at 9.

We can use the present simple to talk about timetables and events in the future.

What happens on Thursday?

Questions: *Wh-* + verb.

Now work in pairs. Student A, turn to assignment 1.1. Student B, turn to assignment 1.2; ask Student A questions to complete your timetable.

5   Do the quiz.

Good learning styles

Are you a good learner? Do you have good study habits? Try this quiz and find out.

1

In a workshop or seminar do you ...

A keep quiet and listen?

B try to share your ideas and opinions?

2

Before a class do you ...

A check you have everything (books, homework and so on)?

B go home quickly?

3

When you are learning something new do you ...

A look for the correct answer?

B look for a number of possible answers?

4

Do you prefer to ...

A study for exams?

B study for pleasure?

5

Do you find learning ...

A frustrating sometimes?

B easy?

Now turn to assignment 1.3 and read your results.

6   Work in pairs. Discuss your results.

10 7   Listen to a seminar and circle A–C.

1 The leader of the seminar is studying ...

A education.

B educational psychology.

C psychology.

2 Intelligent people ...

A do well in their education without making an effort.

B do not do as well as they could without good study habits.

C do not need good study habits.

3 For every class hour students should study _____ additional hours.

  A two   B three   C four

4 Students should …

  A help other students.

  B make sure they organise information.

  C be responsible for their own learning.

5 After class students should …

  A discuss the main points of the class with another student.

  B read the notes on the website.

  C read materials on the reading list.

10 **Now listen again. Complete the notes with no more than three words for each answer.**

Good study habits

The seminar is about the characteristics of (1) _____ .
Students (2) _____ should spend at least three hours studying
alone. On a (3) _____ this is nine hours per week. It is
important to attend classes. Classes help to (4) _____ and
students' learning and are where (5) _____ are explained and
(6) _____ are given.

    Students should try to take (7) _____ in the class – not
just sit quietly. Getting involved, (8) _____ and taking part in
discussion makes learning interesting and helps understanding
(9) _____ .

    Students whose first language is not English have (10) _____
if they prepare before the class. Students should make sure they
read the books on the (11) _____ , read notes on the
(12) _____ and have questions ready.

    After class: go over your notes and see if you can
(13) _____ you own examples. Talk about the class with other
students or use your notes to (14) _____ each other. More
importantly, prepare questions about points you didn't understand
to ask (15) _____ the questions later.

Now work in pairs. List three more good study habits.

Writing

IELTS tasks: task 1 – introducing a report

1 **Work in pairs. Put the subjects in F into groups.**

  1 arts:

  2 sciences:

  3 social sciences:

F

medicine
biology
agriculture
computing
engineering
business
art and design
languages
physics
architecture

G

line graph
bar chart
flow chart
table
pie chart

2 **Label 1–5. Use the words in G.**

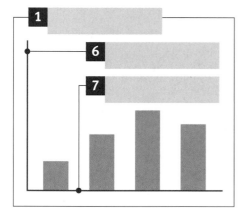

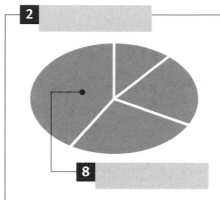

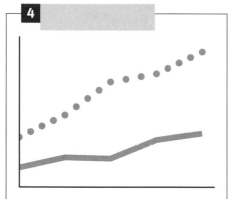

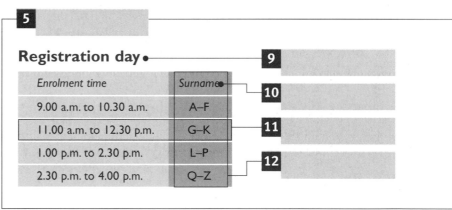

Now label 6–12. Use the words in H.

3 **Look at the charts on the following page and answer the questions.**

  1 What do the charts show?

  2 What number of students took science subjects in 2003?

  3 What percentage of students took business and administration in 2003?

  4 What information is shown in line graphs, but not in pie charts?

  5 Which subject(s) would you like to take and why?

H

row
section/segment
column
horizontal axis
vertical axis
heading
sub-heading

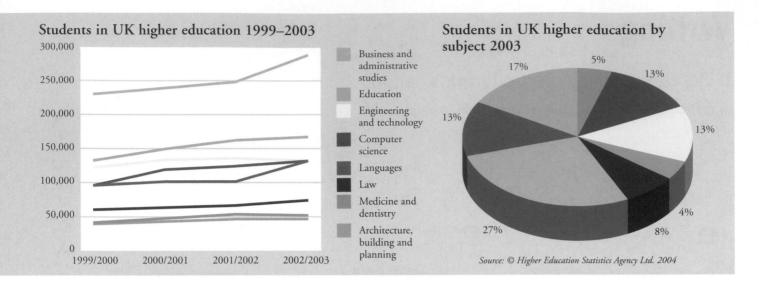

Students in UK higher education 1999–2003

Business and administrative studies
Education
Engineering and technology
Computer science
Languages
Law
Medicine and dentistry
Architecture, building and planning

Students in UK higher education by subject 2003

Source: © Higher Education Statistics Agency Ltd. 2004

4   Look at the charts in 3 again and complete the sentences.

1   The _____ shows the _____ of students by subject area in higher education. We can see from the largest _____ that the greatest number of students are taking _____ studies.

2   The _____ shows the numbers of students by subject over a period of four years. The _____ shows the number of students while the _____ shows the _____ in years.

Achieve IELTS: referring to titles

The title of a graph or chart is given in the writing task. Be careful not to repeat it word for word in your report; try to use your own words.

---

5   Read the title and underline the key words.

> The chart below shows the number of students in Australia by subject in 2003 and 2002. Write a report for a university lecturer describing the information shown below.

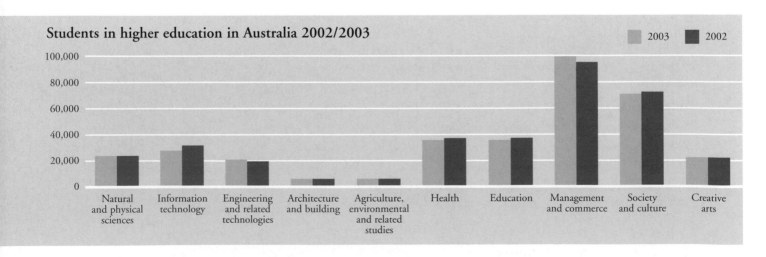

Students in higher education in Australia 2002/2003

Now write the introduction to your report.

Getting around

1 Look at the pictures and answer the questions.

1 Which is a campus university and which is a city university?
2 What differences are there between campus and city universities?

2 Match the places with the definitions.

1 the bursar's office   a students pay their fees here
2 the admissions office   b the restaurant of the university
3 the international office   c paintings and drawings are shown here
4 the refectory   d people that offer students a place at
                                    the university work here
5 the art gallery   e students meet here, go to student
                                    societies and the student shop
6 the Students' Union   f the office for students from abroad

**11   Now listen to three conversations and label
Map A. Start from the Richmond building.**

12 3 Listen to a conversation and circle A–C.

1 The person is …
   A at the university for a tour.
   B at the university for an interview.
   C at the university to meet her tutor.
2 The people are at …
   A the Phoenix building.
   B the Students' Union.
   C the Richmond building.
3 The person is going to …
   A the bursar's office.
   B the Department of Pharmacology.
   C the international office.

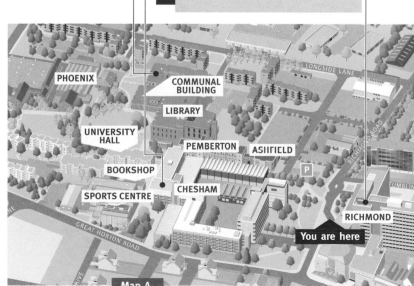

Map A

Express yourself: asking for repetition

13 Listen and underline the stressed words.

Sorry, could you repeat that last sentence?   *Can you say that again?*
Sorry, I didn't quite catch that.   *Did you say go left across the park?*

13 **Now listen again and practise.**

Language study: giving directions

4 **Study the examples and explanation.**

> *Follow the signs to the library, then turn right .*
> *Don't go across the grass.*
>
> **We use (do not/don't) base verb + preposition to give directions. We often use landmarks to give directions.**

A

across
to
forward
towards
between
past

Now complete the sentences. Use the words in A.

From the Phoenix building, walk (1) _____ the park (2) _____ the library. When you get (3) _____ the library, turn right. Go (4) _____ University Hall and the Chesham building and go (5) _____ the Chesham building. Go straight (6) _____ and it's on your right.

B

get to
head for
tell me the way
go straight ahead

5 **Complete the conversation. Use the words and phrases in B.**

A   Excuse me, can you (1) _____ to the Brunei Gallery?

B   Yes, of course. Now, we're here at the Union building. You need to (2) _____ the Senate House, that's the tall, white building.

A   Yes, I see.

B   Go down Malet Street till you (3) _____ Montague Street.

A   Okay.

B   Turn left and go past Senate House to Russell Square, turn left and (4) _____ down Thornhaugh Street.

A   Okay, got that.

B   And the gallery is on your left.

Pronunciation

14 **6** **Listen and notice how the voice rises and falls.**

14 **Now listen again and practise.**

7 **Work in pairs. Use Map B and have a similar conversation.**

Map B

GORDON SQUARE · WOBURN SQUARE · Percival David Foundation of Chinese Art · WOBURN PLACE · CORAN STREET · HERBRAND STREET · BEDFORD WAY · RUSSELL SQUARE CAMPUS · Russell Square · University of London Union · Library · Language Centre · THORNHAUGH STREET · Main Entrance · MALET STREET · Senate House · RUSSELL SQUARE · MONTAGUE STREET · Student Health Centre · The British Museum

Reading

IELTS tasks: matching headings and paragraphs; classification

1 **Work in pairs. Answer the questions.**

1 How many private universities are in your country?

2 Which are the oldest universities?

3 Which British universities do you know?

2 **The reading passage has six sections A–F. Choose the most suitable headings for sections A–F from the list of headings.**

1 Section A _____

2 Section B _____

3 Section C _____

4 Section D ___vii___

5 Section E _____

6 Section F _____

> **List of headings**
>
> i   Campus types
> ii   Old universities
> iii Universities during the industrial revolution
> iv   University colleges
> v   Rising standards in higher education
> vi   The second expansion
> vii Former polytechnics

Universities in Britain

A Today in Britain there are 124 state universities, but only one private university – the University of Buckingham. Before the 19th century there were only six universities: Oxford, Cambridge, Aberdeen, Edinburgh, Glasgow and St Andrews. Universities were
5 usually linked to the Church and were established between the 13th and 15th centuries. They often have good reputations, beautiful old buildings, traditions and usually offer a wide range of courses.

B A number of universities were established in the 19th and early
10 20th centuries as a result of the industrial revolution and they began training highly skilled people for industry. These universities were generally established in major industrial centres such as Birmingham, Manchester, Newcastle and other big cities. Sometimes called modern or civic universities, these universities have the
15 advantage of well-established libraries, academic specialities and accommodation that is close to campus. These universities are often able to provide accommodation for all first year students.

C A number of new universities were established in the 1960s when children born after World War 2 entered the higher education
20 system. The government decided to expand higher education to educate these students. The advantage of these universities is that they are well planned and most of the living and teaching facilities are on campus.

Map labels: Aberdeen, St Andrews, Glasgow, Edinburgh, Newcastle, Manchester, Birmingham, Cambridge, Oxford, London

D Before 1992, higher education in the UK was split into polytechnics and universities. The
25 polytechnics provided skilled people for the industries situated in their region – they
focused on vocational and professional subjects. For many years, polytechnics didn't have
the same influence as universities. However, by 1992, educational standards in polytechnics
were as good as universities and many became universities. Many of these universities also
offer diploma courses.

E These universities are made of several smaller colleges which come together to form a
single university under a senate committee. There are only seven of these institutions in
the UK – London University, Oxford and Cambridge are examples. Specialist colleges offer
a range of courses in one discipline – for example agriculture, music, design or medicine.
Some of these colleges may only offer postgraduate programmes. These colleges are usually
35 small, with a limited number of students.

F Universities have different locations. The older universities often have teaching facilities and
student accommodation situated close together. Students in these usually socialise in a
particular part of the city and there is a strong sense of community despite being in a large
city. Some city campuses are situated on the outskirts of the city. These very often have the
40 space to provide sports facilities and accommodation. They are also close enough to the
city for students to enjoy city life. Some universities, notably Oxford and Cambridge, have
a collegiate structure – that is, students are members of colleges within the university.
These colleges are the centre of social life and academic life. Academic staff usually live at
the college, and students and staff enjoy easy relationships.

3 **Answer the questions using no more than three words from the passage for each question.**

1 Why were several universities established during the 19th and 20th centuries?

2 What did the government decide to do in the 1960s?

3 What qualification do many former polytechnics provide?

4 What are colleges the centre of?

4 **Classify the following descriptions as referring to ...**

OU (old universities)

CU (civic universities)

NU (new universities)

FP (former polytechnics)

UC (university colleges)

NB You may use any answer more than once.

1 _____ have accommodation and educational facilities on campus.

2 _____ provide various courses on a single subject.

3 _____ have lecturers and students living in the same place.

4 _____ were linked to religious institutions.

5 _____ were built in growing cities.

6 _____ offer diploma courses.

5 **Work in pairs. Discuss the questions.**

1 How many ways can you classify universities in your country?

2 Which kind of university is popular in your country?

Language study: general amounts

6 **Study the examples and explanation.**

> *A **number of** universities were established in the 19th and early 20th centuries.*
> ***Many of** these universities also offer diploma courses.*
> ***Some of** these colleges may only offer postgraduate programmes.*
> **When we classify a group of things into type or class, we do not need to give details about numbers. We give a general idea only.**

Now order the phrases in C.

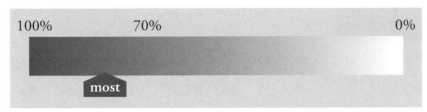

100%   70%   0%

most

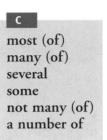

C

most (of)
many (of)
several
some
not many (of)
a number of

7 **Read the passage in 2 again, and underline words and phrases for general amounts.**

Now complete the passage. Use the phrases in C.

University colleges are part of the university world with the same funding and quality control systems. (1) *Most* of [80%] the degrees they offer are in specialist subjects; (2) _____ [60%] have their own degree-awarding powers; and (3) _____ [70%] are specialist institutions. (4) _____ [5%] of them are for postgraduate study only. (5) _____ [80%] colleges are smaller than universities, which means students get a more intimate atmosphere and employment rates are good. An example is The Royal College of Art in London – the world's only postgraduate university of art and design.

8 **Write the questions in full.**

1 Would / like / study abroad?
2 Which country / you like to / to?
3 What / of university / you like to go to: / city, or / university college?

Now add two more questions.

4 _____

5 _____

9 **Ask five students the questions and note their answers.**

Now write about your findings.

Speaking

IELTS tasks: individual long turn – introducing a topic; rounding-off questions (1)

1 **Work in pairs. Tick the phrases that are suitable to introduce a topic and put a cross next to the phrases that are not suitable.**

- [ ] I'd like to talk about my …
- [ ] Listen up …
- [ ] The place I've chosen to talk about is …
- [ ] I'm currently studying at … , so I'll talk about that …
- [ ] I'd like to introduce the topic of a place I have studied …
- [ ] I'm going to speak about …

D

- [ ] number of students in class
- [ ] different courses offered
- [ ] crime
- [ ] the campus
- [ ] entertainment
- [ ] facilities available on campus
- [ ] food
- [ ] student social life

2 **Read the topic and tick the subjects in D that you could talk about.**

> **Part 2: Describe a place where you studied.**
> *You should say:*
> *1 when you studied there*
> *2 what subject you studied*
> *3 why you chose the place*
> *and explain how you benefited from this.*

Now make notes on three of the subjects in D.

3 **Order the questions.**

1 studying you tell Can me a place about you really enjoyed at
2 Why you there go did
3 many with How students you studied

15 **Now listen to an interview and check your answers.**

15 4 **Listen again and note any more rounding-off questions.**

5 **Choose a topic and write two or three rounding-off questions.**

> ● A place you visited.
> ● A course you took.
> ● An interview you went to.

6 **Work in pairs. Student A, use your notes and talk about the topic in 2 for two minutes. Student B, ask Student A the rounding-off questions in activities 3 and 4. Begin *Can you tell me about …***

Now change roles.

Listening

IELTS tasks: labelling; short answers

1 Work in pairs. Decide which facilities in E are at the University Centre and which are at the Students' Union.

🔘 16 Now listen to a talk and check your answers.

🔘 16 2 Listen again and label map C. Use the words and phrases in E and F.

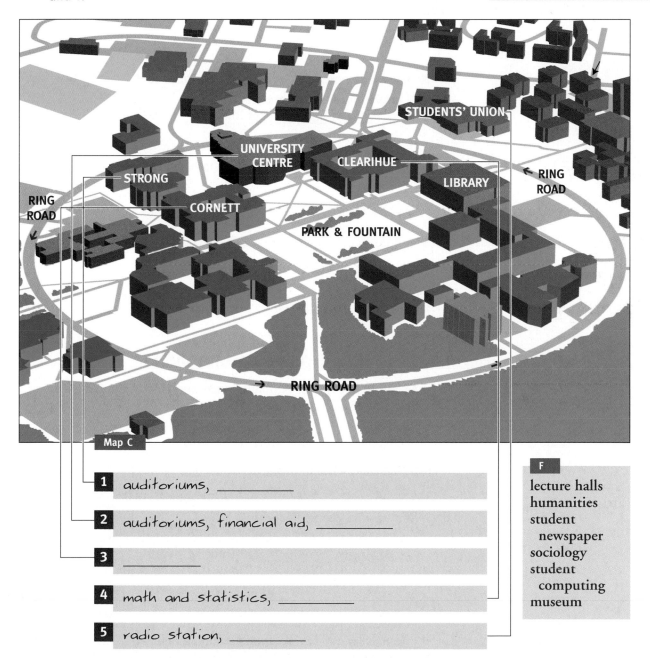

Map C

1 auditoriums, _____

2 auditoriums, financial aid, _____

3 _____

4 math and statistics, _____

5 radio station, _____

3 Label the diagram. Use the words and phrases in G.

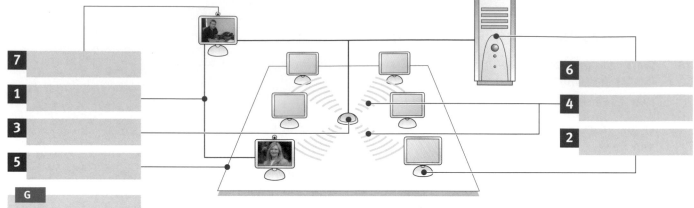

7 _____

1 _____

3 _____

5 _____

6 _____

4 _____

2 _____

G

wireless network
modem
workstation
webcam
video conferencing
server
cluster room

Now work in pairs. Ask each other the questions.

1 Do you often use computers?

2 What do you use them for?

3 How are computers used in education?

17 4 **Listen to a seminar and write OU (Open University) or VC (virtual campus).**

1 short courses in summer _____

2 video conferencing _____

3 watch lectures as they happen _____

4 television and radio programmes _____

17 5 **Listen again and complete the notes. Write no more than three words for each answer.**

The Virtual Campus

VLE = (1) _____

Students could watch

(2) _____ on a webcast.

Video conferencing may

take the place of

(3) _____ .

Advantages:

Number of real students

(4) _____ , number

of virtual students rises.

Students can make

(5) _____ personal.

Disadvantage:

Lose (6) _____ .

Achieve IELTS: repeated information

As the listening test is played once only, the answer may be given twice in the passage.

Students will be able to choose to attend specific lectures and personalise their degree. **What I mean by this is ...**

Other ways of rephrasing are:

I mean to say, what I mean by that is, in other words, that is to say

Now rewrite the sentences.

1 The number of international students entering Australia is growing by 12% each year. In other words ...

2 Students choose their university for many different reasons: for example, course contents or campus type. That is to say ...

6 **Work in pairs. Ask each other the questions.**

1 What kind of university would you like to go to: the Open University, a virtual university, or a 'real' university?

2 Which things influence your choice?

Writing

IELTS tasks: task 1 – describing change

1 Match the words and phrases in H with charts 1–3.

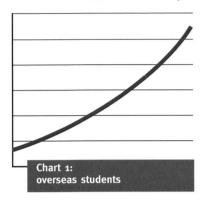

Chart 1:
overseas students

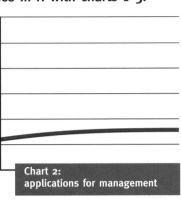

Chart 2:
applications for management

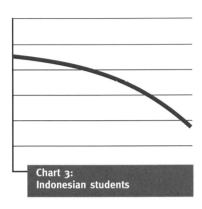

Chart 3:
Indonesian students

H

increase
rise
decrease
drop
fall
reduction
remain stable
levelling-off

2 Complete the sentences. Use the words in I.

1 In the first chart we can see a _____ rise in the number of overseas students.

2 As can be seen in the next chart there was a _____ levelling-off in applications for the management school.

3 As is shown in the last chart there is a _____ decline in students from Indonesia.

I

slow
sharp
slight
dramatic
gradual

Now underline the phrases that introduce the description.

3 Look at charts 4 and 5 and order the sentences.

A The next biggest rise is in students from Korea, rising from 4,300 to 7,000 – a 69 per cent rise.

B As shown in the first chart, there was a sharp rise between 2001 and 2003 in students coming to Australia to study.

C In the second chart we can see the increase by nationality and percentage. The biggest percentage increase was in students from India. The number rose from 2,900 in 2002 to 6,000 in 2003.

D However, if we look at the chart in terms of numbers, the number of students from China is the largest, increasing from 13,500 to 14,200.

E On the other hand, students from Singapore fell by 9 per cent.

F The third largest rise was in students from the United States – up by 17 per cent.

G The charts show the number of overseas students (in thousands) entering Australian universities between 2001 and 2003 overall and according to nationality.

Now work in pairs. Ask each other the questions.

1 Which information did you find interesting?

2 Why do you think so many Americans go to Australia to study?

4 Look at chart 6 and write a short paragraph about student numbers in the UK.

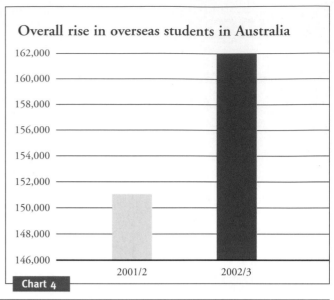

Overall rise in overseas students in Australia

Chart 4

2001/2   2002/3

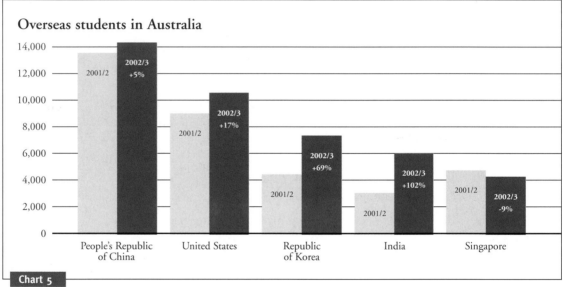

Overseas students in Australia

	2001/2	2002/3
People's Republic of China	2001/2	2002/3 +5%
United States	2001/2	2002/3 +17%
Republic of Korea	2001/2	2002/3 +69%
India	2001/2	2002/3 +102%
Singapore	2001/2	2002/3 -9%

Chart 5

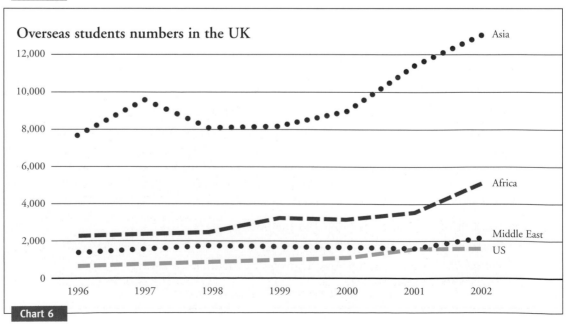

Overseas students numbers in the UK

Asia
Africa
Middle East
US

1996   1997   1998   1999   2000   2001   2002

Chart 6

House share

1   **Name the housework in the picture above. Choose from the words in A.**

2   **Match the words in B with the definitions.**

   1   A person you live with in a flat or house.

   2   Money you give to live in a flat or house.

   3   A person who owns a flat or house and allows people to live there for money.

   4   To divide something into smaller parts.

3   **Do the quiz.**

A	
washing-up	cleaning
vacuuming	making beds
washing	ironing
cooking	DIY (do it yourself)

B	
share	landlord/landlady
rent	flatmate/housemate

FLATMATES QUIZ

Are you easy to live with? Try this quiz and find out.

1 Your flatmate always forgets to wash-up or clean the kitchen. Do you …
A get angry with her?
B quietly tell her you are unhappy about it?
C introduce a cleaning schedule?
D say nothing?

2 Your flatmate is often late paying the rent. How do you react?
A You are understanding; this is an expensive country to live in.
B You are angry; your landlord could throw you out of the flat.
C You are angry; your flatmate promised to pay on time.
D You look for another place to live.

3 When you buy food and drink, you …
A keep your own food locked in a cupboard.
B share things like rice, bread and milk, but keep other things for yourself.
C trust your flatmate to share most things.
D shop and eat together.

4 How do you feel about sharing things like clothes, music and games with a flatmate?
A It's good because you have more variety.
B You don't really want other people using your things.
C People should always ask to borrow your things.
D Sharing always leads to trouble.

5 Would you like a flatmate who …
A often goes out?
B likes to stay in and do the housework?
C is a good friend?
D has lots of friends and loves parties?

Now turn to assignment 3.1 and check your results.

18 4 Listen to a conversation. Which jobs do the students talk about? Circle five letters A–H.

A cleaning the kitchen floor

B ironing

C moving furniture

D washing

E washing-up

F cleaning the bathroom

G shopping

H cutting the grass

18 5 Listen again and answer the questions.

1 What is Ahmed worried about and why?

2 How will Lily go back to the house from the supermarket?

3 Why can't Ahmed help Lily?

Language study: *will* and *going to*

6 Study the examples and explanations.

I'll also buy some soft drinks and juice. I won't be able to help you, I'm afraid.

will/won't (*will not*) + verb

We use *will* for decisions at the time of speaking and predictions about the future.

I'll go with you. I'll help you with that.

We also use *will* for promises and offers.

What are you going to do, Ahmed? I'm going to clean the bathroom.

to be + *going to* + verb

We use *going to* for plans and arrangements.

Now work in groups of three. Each student offers to do three things on the list, then check with the group that everybody knows what they are going to do.

List of things to do

wash the glasses

write invitations

tell the neighbours

blow up balloons

decorate the living room

choose some music

move the furniture

make a salad

prepare some snacks

Listening

IELTS tasks: multiple-choice questions; sentence completion

1   **Work in pairs. Decide which jobs go together with *do*, *make* or *take*.**

_____ the rubbish away ▨   _____ cleaning ▨

_____ the bed ▨   _____ cooking ▨

_____ bottles for recycling ▨   _____ gardening ▨

_____ washing-up ▨   _____ tidying up ▨

19   **Now listen to the conversation and tick the jobs you hear.**

19   2   **Listen again and circle A–D.**

1   Keiko thinks the person with the guitar …
A   was sitting near the door.
B   didn't want to speak to her.
C   talks too much.
D   spilt something.

2   The empty bottles need …
A   washing.
B   throwing away.
C   recycling.
D   putting in the kitchen.

3   Keiko thinks that Ahmed is …
A   lazy.
B   ill.
C   clever.
D   a bad cook.

Express yourself: talking about untidiness

20   **Listen and underline the stressed words.**

Look at the state of this place.   *What a mess.*   *It's so untidy.*   *It's an absolute tip.*

20   **Now listen again and practise.**

Language study: *must(n't)*, *have to* and *need to*

3   **Study the examples and explanations.**

> *… you must do some things for yourself.*
> *He's coming to collect the rent today, so we have to tidy up.*
>
> **We use *must* for an order from another person or from the speaker. We use *have to* when the order is indirect – for example, from an organisation or rules. There is no past tense of *must*. To talk about the past, we use *had to*.**
>
> subject + *must* (*n't*) + verb   subject + *have to* + verb
>
> *We also need to clean up the stain.*
>
> **We use *need to* when something is necessary.**

Now complete the sentences.

1 Landlord to students: This room is a mess. You _____ clean it immediately.

2 Lily to Keiko: The landlord is very angry. We _____ clean the living room before he comes back.

3 Keiko to Lily: OK, I'll get the vacuum cleaner. But we _____ clean the kitchen, because I did it yesterday. Do we _____ clean the bathroom?

4 Work in pairs. Ask each other which jobs in the house you have to do today.

5 Put the words in C into groups.

1 accommodation:
2 places in a hall:
3 people working in a hall:

21 Now listen to the accommodation officer giving a talk to new students. Tick the words in C you hear.

21 6 Listen again and complete the sentences. Write no more than three words for each space.

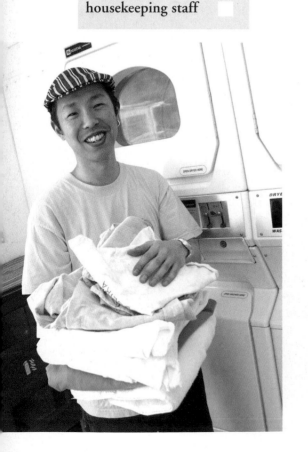

> Hall rules
>
> Students must stay in a (1) _____ for the first six months. The halls have a (2) _____ kitchen with lockable cupboards. You must buy a (3) _____ if you want a television. Letters and parcels can be collected from the (4) _____. You can do your washing and ironing in the (5) _____. The (6) _____ staff will give you clean sheets every week. The (7) _____ name is John Hawes. Dialling the number zero on the internal phones will connect you to the (8) _____. The cheapest kind of rented place is a (9) _____. Check the noticeboard if you would like to move into a (10) _____.

7 Work in pairs. Ask each other the questions.

1 Which kind of accommodation would you like to live in?
2 What are the advantages and disadvantages of each one?

Reading

1 **Tick who usually does these jobs in the house.**

	a man	a woman	both	Who? (sister, mother, wife, father...)
washing-up				
vacuuming				
ironing				
washing				
cooking				
cleaning				
making beds				
DIY				

Now discuss the questions.

1 Is there a fair balance between the housework that men and women family members do in your country?

2 Why/why not?

2 **Work in pairs. Read the title of the passage and guess the reasons for it.**

An equal share of housework makes a happy relationship

A recent study shows that an unequal share of household chores is still the norm in many households, despite the fact that many more women now have jobs. In a survey of 1,256 people aged between 18 and 65, men said they contributed an average of 37 per cent of the total housework, while the women estimated their share to be nearly
5 double that, at 70 per cent. This ratio was not affected by whether the woman was working or not.

When they were asked what they thought is a fair division of labour, women with jobs felt that housework should be shared equally between male and female partners. Women who did not work outside the home were satisfied to perform 80 per cent –
10 the majority of the household work, if their husbands did the remainder. Research has shown that, if levels increase beyond these percentages, women become unhappy and anxious, and feel they are unimportant.

After marriage, a woman is reported to increase her household workload by 14 hours per week, but for men the amount is just 90 minutes. So the division of labour becomes unbalanced, as the man's share increases much less than the woman's. It is the inequality and loss of respect, not the actual number of hours, which leads to anxiety and depression. The research describes housework as thankless and unfulfilling. Activities included in the study were cooking, cleaning, shopping, doing laundry, washing-up and childcare. Women who have jobs report that they feel overworked by these chores in addition to their professional duties. In contrast, full-time homemakers frequently anticipate going back to work when the children grow up. Distress for this group is caused by losing the teamwork in the marriage.

In cases where men perform most of the housework, results were similar. The men also became depressed by the imbalance of labour. The research showed that the least distressed people are those who have an equal share, implying that men could perform significantly more of the chores and even benefit from this. The research concludes, 'Everybody benefits from sharing the housework. Even for women keeping house, a shared division of labour is important. If you decide to stay at home to raise the children, you don't want to become the servant of the house.'

Now read the passage. Do the statements reflect the claims of the writer?

Write: YES if the statement reflects the claims of the writer.
   NO if the statement contradicts the claims of the writer.
   NOT GIVEN if it is impossible to say what the writer thinks about this.

1   The people in the survey were all married couples. _____
2   Working women do more housework than their partners. _____
3   People who do too many hours of housework become depressed. _____
4   Women with jobs think they are working too hard because of the additional housework. _____
5   Men become ill if they do an equal share. _____

3   Read the passage again and circle one letter A–D.

1   After they get married …
   A   men do less housework.
   B   women do twice as much housework.
   C   men do more housework.
   D   women have a bigger house.

2   Working women …
   A   do 80 per cent of the housework.
   B   want their partners to do an equal share.
   C   would prefer not to have a job.
   D   are anxious and depressed.

3   Women who do not have jobs become depressed …
   A   if their husbands do 20 per cent of the chores.
   B   if they have to do more than half the housework.
   C   because they have no self-respect.
   D   when their husbands do not help them.

4   **Complete the summary. Choose no more than two words or a number from the reading passage for each answer.**

In most households, (1) _____ do more housework than (2) _____ . Although working women think men should share the housework (3) _____ , those who don't have a paid job agree to do (4) _____ of the chores. When a woman gets married, her workload usually (5) _____ to 14 hours per week. When their children grow up, homemakers often want to get (6) _____ and when their husbands do not help them at home, they feel there is no more (7) _____ in their marriages. Men also feel depressed if they have to do too much housework. The happiest couples are those who (8) _____ the housework.

5   **Match the definitions with the words in D.**

1   to guess the amount or time of something
2   one amount compared to another group
3   to cut something into smaller parts and share it
4   what usually happens
5   what is left of an amount after something is taken away

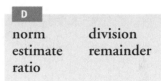

> **D**
>
> norm   division
> estimate   remainder
> ratio

6   **Make opposites with the words in E. Use these prefixes.**

> un-   in-

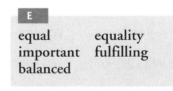

> **E**
>
> equal   equality
> important   fulfilling
> balanced

7   **Look at the example and complete the chart for yourself. Use the words in F.**

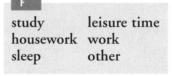

> **F**
>
> study   leisure time
> housework   work
> sleep   other

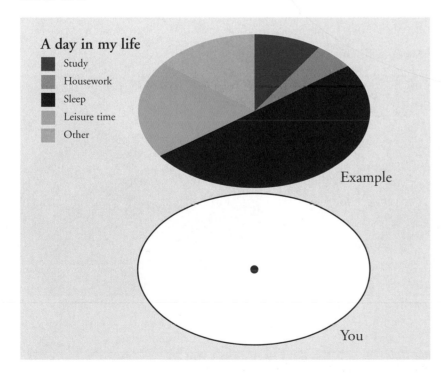

A day in my life
- Study
- Housework
- Sleep
- Leisure time
- Other

Example

You

Now work in pairs. Compare and discuss your charts.

Speaking

IELTS tasks: individual long turn – giving personal information

1 Match the words in G with the pictures.

A

B

D

C

Now work in pairs. Decide which is the most important feature of a house.

location   number of rooms   space   garden   age

2 Describe the pictures with the words in H.

A

B

Pronunciation

22 **3** Listen and notice how we say the final -*y* in these words.

messy   cosy   gloomy   tidy   stuffy   airy

22 Now listen again and practise.

23 **4**   Listen and label the plan with the words in I.

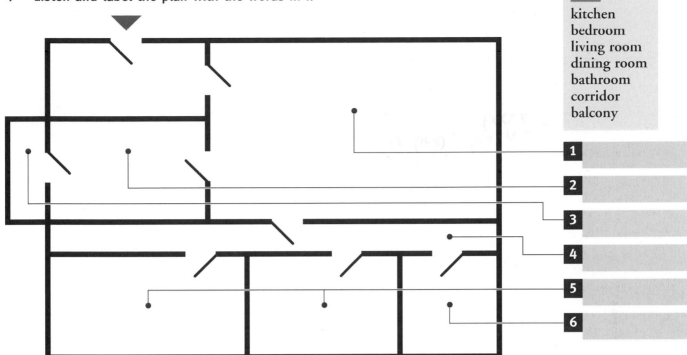

I

kitchen
bedroom
living room
dining room
bathroom
corridor
balcony

1
2
3
4
5
6

Achieve IELTS: talking about your home

One of the questions examiners often ask is about your home. It may be a short question, near to the beginning of the interview. The examiner may ask ...

What type of accommodation do you live in? What is it like?

How many people do you live with? Where do you go shopping?

Now write three more questions about people's homes.

---

5   Read the topic and make notes.

Part 2: Describe a place you enjoyed living.

You should say:

1 *which area it is in*

2 *how many people live with you*

3 *what it is like.*

You should also explain why you like or dislike living there.

Now work in pairs. Take turns to talk about the topic.

Writing

IELTS tasks: task 1 – task achievement

1   Work in pairs. Ask each other the questions.

1   Do you think most students know how to look after themselves when they first start university?

2   Can you cook for yourself or do you prefer fast food?

2   Look at the chart and answer the questions.

1   What does the chart show?

2   What percentage of male students can wash clothes?

3   What percentage of female students know how to cook?

4   What percentage of male students know how to iron their clothes?

3   Look at the chart and read the description. Decide which information is ...

1   wrong or inaccurate.   2   missing.   3   not useful or irrelevant.

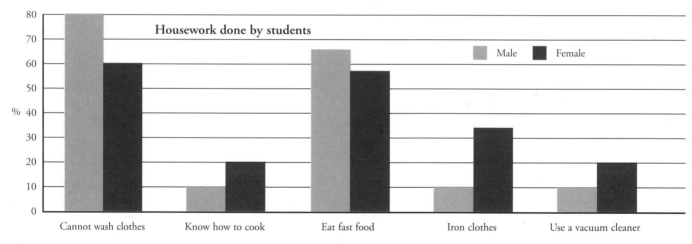

The chart shows the results of some students who were interviewed about their ability to live away from home. It also shows the differences between male and female students. We can see that 80 per cent of male students did not know how to wash clothes, while the percentage of females who could not do laundry was 25 per cent less. Female students have a lot more clothes than males. Not many students could cook for themselves: only 10 per cent of the males and 20 per cent of the females. The majority of female students eat fast food instead of cooking, and even more males live on fast food: almost two out of three do this. There are many fast food outlets around the campus. Very few male students know how to iron their clothes, but 20 per cent of females knew how to operate a vacuum cleaner. Vacuum cleaners use a lot of electricity.

Now rewrite the description in 3.

4　**Write questions about housework for the other students.**

Do you know how to wash clothes?

Do you know how to cook?

Can you iron clothes?

Now ask ten students your questions.

5　**Put the information into a chart and write a short description.**

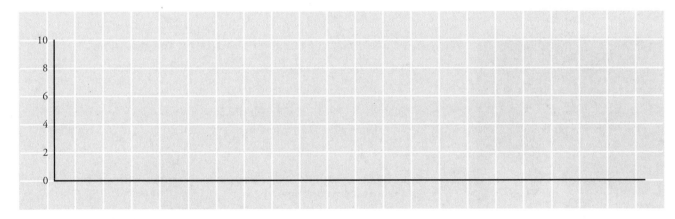

UNIT 4
Film society

Let's catch a film

documentary
drama
biography
docudrama

1   Match the definitions with the words in A.

1   a film about a fictional story
2   a film that includes drama and documentary
3   a film about someone's life
4   a film about real life

24   2   Listen to a conversation and answer the questions.

1   What is *Touching the Void* about?
2   What kind of film is it?
3   What kind of reviews did it get?
4   Why does Tao want to see the film?
5   What did Catherine think of the film?

24   3   Listen again and complete each sentence with no more than three words or a number.

City of God is a film about (1) _____ in a slum town in Brazil.
In *Touching the Void*, what happened after a climbing disaster in
(2) _____ . The cinema opens (3) _____ . There's 15
minutes for (4) _____ . The film starts (5) _____ . The film
lasts (6) _____ . Per cent discount with student card:
(7) _____ . There's an extra discount for (8) _____ .

Now circle the correct letter A–C.

1   The scene Catherine liked best was …
    A   when Joe and Simon were climbing the mountain.
    B   when Joe and Simon were telling their story.
    C   when they were sleeping and heard Joe shouting.

2 The scene Tao liked was …

   A when Joe and Simon were telling their story.

   B when Simon was lowering Joe down the mountain.

   C when Simon made a difficult decision.

Express yourself: talking about films

(25) **Listen and underline the stressed words.**

It's really exciting.   *How good was that?*

I really enjoyed it   *it's a great film.*

(25) **Now listen again and practise.**

Language study: narrative tenses

4   **Study the examples and explanations.**

> *I really **enjoyed** it. Joe **broke** his leg.*
>
> **We use the past tense to talk about completed actions in the past. Regular verbs take *-ed*. Some past tense verbs are irregular: break ➤ broke.**
>
> *They **were climbing** the mountain really quickly.*
>
> **We use the past continuous when we give background information.**
>
> *was/were + (not) + verb(-ing)*
>
> *They **were sleeping** at the camp when they **heard** Joe calling.*
>
> **We use the past simple with the past continuous to show one event happening in the middle of a longer event.**

Now complete the sentences.

1 As Simon and Joe _____ the mountain an avalanche
   _____ . (approach/occur)

2 When they _____ along the top of the mountain, they
   _____ accidents other climbers had. (walk/remember)

3 As Joe _____ he _____ and _____ his leg.
   (walk/fall/break)

4 Simon _____ Joe down the mountain when Joe accidentally
   _____ over the edge. (lower/go)

5   **Work in pairs. Ask each other the questions.**

1 Which film can you remember best?

2 What kind of film is it?

3 What scene can you remember best and what happened in
   the scene?

Reading

IELTS tasks: true/false/not given; multiple-choice questions

1 Work in pairs. Answer the questions.

1 What do students study in Media Studies?
2 Why do you think it is a popular subject in Britain?
3 Would you like to do Media Studies?

Now use the reading passage 'Welcome to the Media, Film and Cultural Studies course' to check your answer to the first question.

Welcome to the Media, Film and Cultural Studies course ...

The course introduces you to key ideas in Cultural Studies and the study of film. During the course we consider competing definitions of the terms *culture* and *media*, and we explore a range of cultural material from a variety of media. We look at the ways in which the cultural environment shapes our beliefs and values. While we assume that the meaning of much of the cultural material around us is obvious and transparent, this course demonstrates that we are constantly interpreting films, newspapers, adverts, music and videos.

We will examine the way in which media and institutions transmit ideas and values. This will be explored through an examination of the importance of brands and fashion in consumer culture.

B

examine
demonstrate
consider
assume

2 Find the words in B in the text and choose the definition.

1 to think about something
2 to show clearly that something is true
3 to question something in order to understand it
4 to believe something is true

3 Read the passage in 1 again.

Write: **TRUE** if the statement is true according to the passage.
FALSE if the statement is false according to the passage.
NOT GIVEN if the statement is not given in the passage.

1 There is more than one definition of culture.   _____
2 The course concentrates on one kind of media.   _____
3 People think the meaning of culture is obvious, but
  in fact it is not.   _____
4 Television is the most important form of media today.   _____
5 Brands and fashions are unimportant in today's culture. _____

4 Work in pairs. Ask each other the questions.

1 Do you think Media Studies is an interesting or important subject?
2 Do you think Media Studies helps people to understand the world around us?
3 Should children be taught Media Studies? Why?/Why not?

5 Read the passage below and choose the most suitable title A–E.

A Product placement
B Media studies for children
C The danger of too much TV
D Marketing and young viewers
E The British Film Institute

Media Studies is more popular than ever in lecture halls across the country. Last year saw a rise of 15.8 per cent in the number of students on such
5 courses. In future, however, children as young as three may be learning in the most basic way the sort of skills that are taught on such courses. Media literacy is the buzzword. Already part
10 of the national curriculum in England for older children, the government also wants primary school pupils to have a greater understanding of TV, films and other media. More than ever before,
15 children are living in a media-filled world and exposed to television in particular. A third of children under the age of four have a TV in their bedroom, as do more than half of under-16 year-olds. On average, children spend
20 two-and-a-half hours a day watching 'the box'.

With this trend comes growing concern about how children are affected by what they see. When companies pay to have their brands appear within a programme, this is *product placement*, and it is just
25 one of the things children may need to know more about, according to the government's Culture Secretary. Although product placement is banned for programme makers in Britain, on commercial TV as well as the BBC, it is increasingly used in
30 films and can be found on the small screen through imported programmes such as *Friends*, which, for example, has used *Oreo* cookies to good effect. Some international companies have made programmes which, although not using their brand
35 names, focused heavily on products associated with them. In the film *Matrix Reloaded* Samsung mobile phones are often shown – Samsung reportedly paid US $100 million for this.

40 A parliamentary investigation into tobacco promotion shed light on the particularly clever minds of some marketing people. For example, one marketer asked if the logo of a Formula
45 One racing team could be changed to include a symbol from a well-known cigarette brand. With the rise of digital TV, which enables viewers to skip commercial breaks, some experts say
50 advertisers might need to be increasingly creative about ways to get their message across.

Under the government's new plans, children could be taught to understand the increasingly
55 complex media. A guide from the British Film Institute sets out priorities for teaching three to 11-year-olds. It reads: 'It is important to encourage children to distinguish between different forms of media such as documentary, news and
60 advertisements, and to recognise that the source of a text can make a difference to the truth or accuracy of what it says.'

Despite this, the British Film Institute's Cary Bazalgette rejects the term *media studies* in favour
65 of *media literacy*. Its aims are no different from reading classes, she says. 'It's about building up children's confidence as readers. We're saying to teachers you can now build that up with media forms children are already familiar with. You cannot
70 be literate in the 21st century unless you are literate in all the media that are used to communicate.'

6 **Read the passage again and circle the appropriate letters A–D.**

1 The government wants to introduce media studies for …
A teachers.
B young children.
C children who spend a lot of time watching TV.
D children who have a TV in their bedroom.

2 Product placement is …
A not allowed for people making programmes in Britain.
B advertising before a film or television programme.
C something children can ignore.
D companies making television programmes showing their own brand names.

3 Advertisers need to be creative …
A to avoid investigation by parliament.
B because they have clever minds.
C to persuade Formula One teams to change their symbols.
D to communicate with the viewers without using commercial breaks.

4 The British Film Institute wants three to 11-year-old children …
A to learn media literacy, not media studies.
B to be able to read better.
C to be able to understand documentaries.
D to understand that the source of the text influences the message.

7 **Read the statements and tick the ones you agree with.**

1 It is all right for children to spend two-and-a-half hours a day watching TV.
2 Product placement does not influence people.
3 It is important to recognise that the source of a text can influence the information in it.
4 You cannot be literate in the 21st century unless you are literate in all the media.

Now work in pairs. Discuss and give reasons for your answers.

Listening

IELTS tasks: table completion; short answers

1   **Work in pairs. Answer the questions.**

   1   Are you a member of a club or society?
   2   Do you go to meetings?
   3   Do you like meetings?

2   **Match the words with the definitions.**

   1   minutes   a   what will be discussed at this meeting
   2   apologies   b   anything else people want to discuss
                                 (any other business)
   3   aob   c   what happened in the last meeting
   4   item 1, 2, 3 …   d   who cannot come to the meeting

3   **Put the agenda items in 2 in order.**

🔘26   **Now listen to a meeting and check your answers.**

4   **Label the diagram. Use the words in C.**

C

events organiser
committee
secretary
treasurer

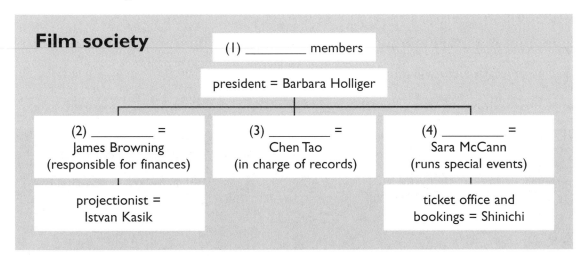

Film society

(1) _____ members

president = Barbara Holliger

(2) _____ =
James Browning
(responsible for finances)

(3) _____ =
Chen Tao
(in charge of records)

(4) _____ =
Sara McCann
(runs special events)

projectionist =
Istvan Kasik

ticket office and
bookings = Shinichi

🔘26   5   **Listen again. Complete the agenda.**

Film society: meeting agenda

1   _____
   Shin: reason _____
   Tao: reason _____

2   Minutes of last meeting
   approved: YES/NO
   objections: YES/NO

3   Item 1: state of the _____
   Item 2: organise a _____

4   AOB

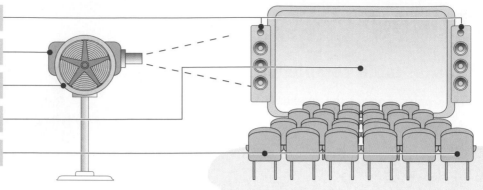
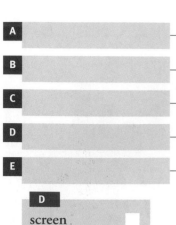

A

B

C

D

E

screen ☐
seats ☐
sound system ☐
projector ☐
film ☐

6 **Label the picture. Use the words in D.**

(27) **Now listen and tick the things you hear.**

(27) **7** **Listen again. Circle three letters A–E.**

1 Istvan checks …
 A the quality of the sound.
 B the projector.
 C the screen.
 D the chairs.
 E the state of the film from the distributors.

Now complete the sentences.

The cost of replacing the screen is (1) _____ . The film society
needs to raise about (2) _____ .

8 **Label the pictures. Choose from the words in E.**

E

thriller
horror
comedy
romantic
science fiction
martial arts

A

B

C

(28) **Now listen and circle the correct letters A–C.**

1 James suggests a …
 A horror film. B martial arts film. C science fiction film.

2 Dona likes Sara's idea for a …
 A film quiz. B raffle. C costume competition.

3 Dona doesn't want more money from the Students' Union because …
 A she doesn't like asking for money.
 B the Film Society traditionally makes money for the Union.
 C she wants to raise the money alone.

9   Match the verbs with the nouns.

1	approve	a	the next item
2	send	b	funds
3	raise	c	a vote
4	move on to	d	the minutes
5	have	e	an apology

Language study: suggestions

10   Study the examples and explanations.

> *your thoughts on this ... any suggestions about ... Like ...?*
> *What's the position with ...? Any more suggestions?*
>
> **We use these phrases to ask for suggestions.**
>
> *How about ... I'd like to suggest ... We could ...*
>
> **We use these phrases to make suggestions.**
>
> *I'd like to avoid doing that ...*
>
> **When we decline a suggestion we usually give a reason.**

Now complete the sentences.

1   ... now for the fund-raising event. _____ anybody?

2   I'd _____ a charity walk.

3   Isn't that a bit boring? Let's do something fun. _____ climbing the Senate house?

4   I think we should _____ . We don't want to get into trouble.

29   11   Listen and check your answers.

Pronunciation

29   12   Listen again and practise.

13   Work in pairs. Student A, you are the President of the Film society – read your role card. Student B, you are the Events organiser – read your role card.

Student A	**Student B**
President of the Film society	Events organiser of the Film society
● Ask for a suggestion for a film next week.	● Give a suggestion for a film next week.
● Reject Student B's first suggestion and give a reason.	● Disagree with Student A's reason, and make another suggestion.
● Say Student B's next suggestion is interesting, but you would like another idea.	● Make a final suggestion and give a reason for it.
● Accept Student B's last suggestion.	

Now have a conversation using the role cards.

Speaking

IELTS tasks: individual long turn – giving longer answers (1)

1   **Work in groups. Discuss ways to raise funds for a new piece of equipment for a student society. Follow these steps.**

    1   Decide which society you are and which piece of new equipment you need.

    2   Decide who is the president, treasurer and secretary.

    3   Write an agenda.

    4   Think of a suggestion and reasons why it is a good suggestion.

    5   Hold a meeting.

2   **Read the topic below and underline the main points.**

Part 2: Describe a film you saw which made an impression on you.

You should say:

1   what film and what type of film it is

2   when you saw it

3   what your favourite part of the film is

and explain why it made an impression on you.

Now make notes on the main points.

(30) 3   Read the notes, then listen and write ∧ when you hear any extra information.

My favourite film is The Matrix – it's a science fiction film. I saw it a few years ago as soon as it was released. The best part of the film was when the main character was trying to rescue his friend. It made a big impression on me – I liked it very much.

Achieve IELTS: giving longer answers

It is a good idea to give longer answers. This helps the examiner assess your English and helps you to be more fluent.

The Matrix *is a science fiction film,* **but at the same time** *you could call it an action film.*

Other words and phrases for giving longer answers are:

because   in fact   as

Now look at your notes for activity 2 and add reasons.

4   **Work in pairs. Discuss the topic in activity 2.**

Writing

IELTS tasks: task 1 – referring to numbers

1   Match the numbers with the words.

1   1,835,000,000   a   one billion, one hundred and twenty nine million

2   922,379,000   b   four hundred and seventy million, six hundred thousand

3   470,600,000   c   one billion, eight hundred and thirty five million

4   1,129,000,000   d   nine hundred and twenty two million, three hundred and
                                           seventy nine thousand

Now match the numbers with films a–d.

Selection of biggest grossing films to 2004

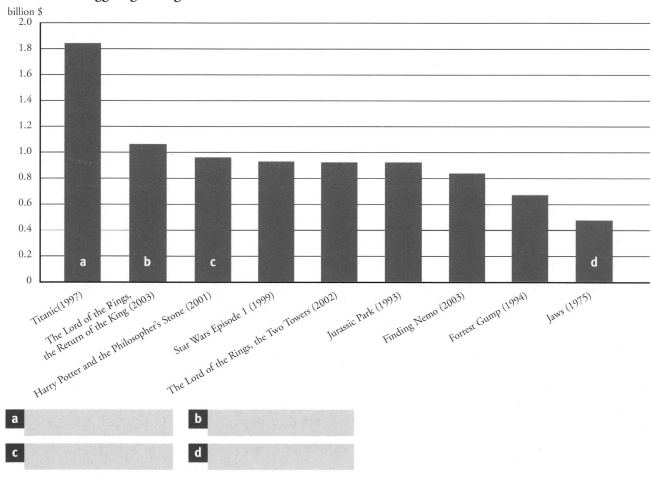

2   Look at the chart and answer the questions.

1   Which film had the second-largest box office earnings?

2   Which films earned roughly half of the highest-earning film?

Now work in pairs. Ask each other the questions.

1   Does any of the information surprise/interest you?

2   Did you see any of these films?

3   Label the charts. Use the words in F.

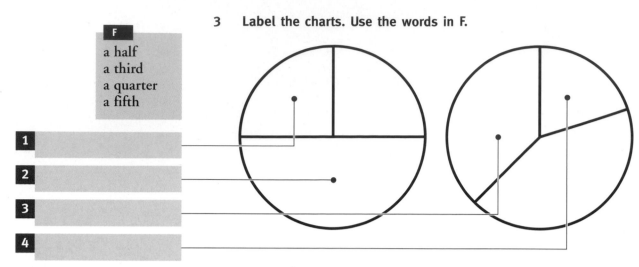

F

a half
a third
a quarter
a fifth

1 _____
2 _____
3 _____
4 _____

Now make sentences.

Forrest Gump	took	roughly	50%/half	of the amount of money of *Titanic*.
Star Wars, episode I		nearly	a third	
Jurassic Park		almost	25%/a quarter	
		approximately		

31   **4**   **Listen to a talk and complete the passage.**

The centre of the film industry is Hollywood in America, which makes (1) _____ the largest amount of money. However, Hollywood is not the biggest producer of films. In fact, this is India which produced (2) _____ films in 1999. The second-largest producer is the USA, which made (3) _____ the amount made in India (4) _____ films. In third position is Japan, which made (5) _____ films in 1999. The next largest producer of films was Italy, which made just (6) _____ , although today Britain may have overtaken Italy in film production.

Now circle the phrases for referring to figures.

5   **Look at the chart in activity 1 and write a paragraph about it.**

CUe FM

1 **Work in pairs. Ask each other these questions.**

   1 When you wake up do you switch on …

     A the kettle?

     B the radio?

     C the TV?

     D nothing (you hate noise in the morning!)?

   2 During the week do you …

     A choose your radio programmes?

     B have the radio on in the background?

     C just listen to music?

     D never listen to radio programmes?

   3 What kind of radio programmes do you listen to? Are they …

     A chart music?

     B chat-show and phone-in programmes?

     C news, reviews and reports?

     D quizzes, competitions and comedy programmes?

2 **Read the passage on the following page and answer the questions.**

   1 What is CUe FM?

   2 When does it broadcast?

   3 What kind of programmes does it broadcast?

   4 How can you join?

CUe FM

CUe FM is the University of Canberra's very own radio station. Tune in, check it out and turn it up. Broadcasting on 87.7FM CUe FM boasts a range of music and entertainment. You can hear CUe FM 24 hours a day with up to 16 hours of live-to-air broadcasting each day. CUe FM programmes cover everything from punk, pop, rock, Australian, metal, dance, funk, Blues, World Music and more, plus news, phone-ins, gossip, discussions and competitions. CUe FM is one of the societies of UCU. This way you can join the club and become a member of the radio station. It will cost AU$10 if you're a UC student and part of your membership gives you a two-hour timeslot for your programme throughout the week.

Want to be a DJ?

Even if you've got no experience at a radio station, we can train you how to do it. All you need to do is choose some tunes from our CD library. For more details contact us via e-mail or visit UCU Member Services.

Now work in pairs. Answer the questions.

1 Would you like to be a DJ? *why / why not.*

2 What kind of programme would you like to broadcast? *give reasons*

32 **3** **Listen and complete the notes. Write no more than three words or a number for each answer.**

> CUe FM Application form
>
> Name: Paul Dyson
> Department: (1) _____
> Interests: (2) ▮ music library
>   DJ
>   technical support
>   other
> UCU number: (3) _____
> Reason for joining: (4) Always been _____
> Experience: (5) DJ   YES/NO
>   (6) Tech support   YES/NO
> News update: (7) Women's rugby _____ !

32 **4** **Listen again and complete the notes. Write no more than three words for each answer.**

> **Paul's favourite radio programme:** the (1) _____
> **Type of music Paul likes:** (2) _____
> **Breakfast slot:** pop and rock with (3) _____ and chat
> **Mid-afternoon:** music (4) _____ and news
> **Evening:** competitions, news and (5) _____ at university
> **Late show:** mostly music with some (6) _____

Express yourself: personal information

33 | **Listen and mark the stressed words.**

... tell me something about yourself.
Well as you probably know ...
... let me tell you a bit about ...

33 | **Now listen again and practise.**

Language study: present perfect (1)

5   **Study the examples and explanations.**

> *Have you (ever) done DJing?*
> *I've watched the other people do it.*
>
> **We use the present perfect when we talk about experiences. Verbs which are irregular in the past tense are also irregular in the present perfect.**
>
> *have (not/n't)* + past participle
>
> *How long have you been at the university?*
> *I've been here for nearly five months.*
>
> **We use *how long* with *for* + length of time or *since* + date to talk about periods of time.**
>
> *I've always been interested in music.*
> *I've never been a DJ.*
> *I've recently become interested in storing music electronically.*
>
> **We use adverbs of time to give more information about an experience.**

Now write the questions in full.

1   Have you / listened / classical music?
2   Have you / / to opera?
3   Have you / wanted to / a DJ?
4   Have you ever / to a pop concert?
5   / you ever / to play a musical instrument?
6   / you / sung for people?

6   **Work in pairs. Ask each other the questions.**

Listening

IELTS tasks: note completion; table completion

1 Match the headlines with the pictures.

A

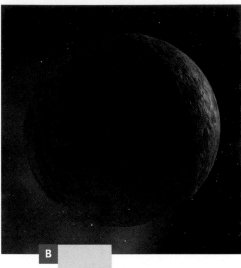

B

C

1   **Music company cuts 1,500 jobs**

2   **South Korea opens high-speed rail link**

3   **New planet discovered**

Now work in pairs. Discuss what the stories are about.

 2   Listen to a news report and order the pictures in activity 1.

     Now listen again and complete the notes. Write no more than three words or a number.

The new planet is as big as Pluto, but is (1) _____ further away and takes (2) _____ to orbit the sun. It's the largest object found since Pluto (3) _____ . Some scientists say it is a (4) _____ – not a real planet.

South Korea has launched the KTX, or (5) _____ . The journey took two hours and 40 minutes, but previously it took (6) _____ hours. The KTX will carry (7) _____ a day.

Music company EMI has cut 1,500 jobs and has dropped (8) _____ of the artists. It is the world's (9) _____ music company. The largest company, Universal, said that job cuts are because of (10) _____ piracy.

3   Work in pairs. Discuss the questions.

1   Which news from activity 2 have you heard?
2   Which did you find interesting?
3   Which would you like to know more about?

Language study: present perfect (2)

4 **Study the examples and explanations.**

> *The project **has cost** US$15.3 billion and **was developed** over 12 years.*
> **We use the present perfect to talk about news. We give details about the news with the past tense.**
>
> *The discovery **has caused** discussion among astronomers about exactly **what is** a planet.*
> **We also use the present perfect to talk about past events which have an effect on the present.**

Now write full sentences for the headlines in 1 and give more details about each story.

5 **Match the words with the definitions.**

1 syndicate   a a business owned by the people who work for it
2 press   b newspapers and news magazines
3 corporation   c a business that provides a service
4 co-operative   d to sell information to broadcasters so it can be shown in different places
5 agency   e a large company or business organisation

35 **6** **Listen and circle the correct letter A–C.**

1 The students are in …   2 Paula talks about …
   A a meeting.   A news gathering.
   B a seminar.   B broadcasting.
   C a lecture.   C information and communications.

3 She gives details about …
   A *The New York Times.*
   B types of press agency.
   C the student radio station.

Now write LO for large organisation, GA for government agency, CO for co-operative, or C for corporation.

1 _____ eg, The New York Times, the BBC   3 _____ eg, Reuters
2 _____ eg, the Associated Press, Kyodo   4 _____ eg, ITAR-TASS

35 **7** **Listen to the seminar again and complete the table.**

Press agencies		
BBC	(1) _____ offices around the world.	
Kyodo	formed in (2) _____ with (3) _____ journalists working for it.	
Reuters	set up in (4) _____ with (5) _____ journalists working for it.	
ITAR-TASS	established (6) _____ with (7) _____ journalists in the late 1980s.	

8 **Work in pairs. Discuss the questions.**

1 How many broadcasters are there in your country?
2 Do any broadcast news only?
3 Are there any press agencies in your country?

Reading

IELTS tasks: multiple-choice questions

1 Order pictures A–D.

Now read the passages and check your answers.

Reuters: the business of news

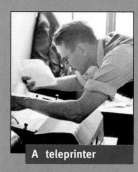

A teleprinter

B monitor dealing service

C stockmaster

D telegraph

A One of the world's biggest suppliers of news and financial information, Reuters Group PLC, has a worldwide network of 2,000 journalists and provides news stories, photographs and video to newspapers, television and Internet sites. Although it is better known as a press agency, Reuters in fact makes most of its profits through
5 financial information such as currency rates and stock prices to bankers and investors all over the world.

B The history of Reuters goes hand in hand with improvements in communication technology. Reuters was established by Paul Julius Reuter – originally a bookseller in Germany, he set up a service using carrier pigeons to fly stock prices between Aachen
10 in Germany, where the German telegraph line ended, and Brussels in Belgium, where the Belgian telegraph line began. In 1851 London had an important place in the global telegraphic network and due to this Reuter moved into an office near the London stock exchange from where he supplied investors in London and Paris with stock prices over the new Dover–Calais telegraph line. He expanded the service to include
15 news items and by the late 1850s had offices throughout Europe.

C As overland and undersea cables were laid, Reuters business expanded to the Far East in 1872 and South America in 1874. Its reputation also grew with a number of scoops – for example, Reuters was the first in Europe to announce President Lincoln's death in 1865. Reuter retired in 1872 and the company changed its name to Reuters Ltd. In
20 1923 Reuters began to use teleprinters to distribute news to London newspapers and to supply news to Europe.

D After increasing pressure from the British government for Reuters to serve British interests, the company was restructured in 1941 in order to maintain its independence as a press agency. At the same time, in the face of competition from
25 American agencies after World War Two, Reuters expanded its financial information services. In 1964 Reuters introduced Stockmaster, which transmitted stock information from around the world onto computer screens. In 1973 the launch of the Reuters monitor created an electronic marketplace for foreign currency by displaying currency rates in real time. Reuters expanded this to include news and other financial
30 information. This was followed by the Reuters monitor dealing service in 1981, which allowed foreign currency traders to trade directly from their own computer.

E In the 1990s Reuters continued to develop information systems including multimedia and online services. It bought a number of companies, including a television company which was called Reuters Television. Reuters Television provides news, sports, business
35 and entertainment via satellite to broadcasters in more than 90 countries. Today's Reuters is still based on its Trust Principles, which state that news and information from the company must be independent and free from bias. Reuters' journalists have to provide accurate and clear descriptions of events so that individuals, organisations and governments can make their own decisions based on facts.

2   Read the passage again. Which paragraphs state the following information?

1   Reuters' influence increased as it was often the first with new news. _____

2   The company changed its structure to avoid government influence. _____

3   Reuters makes most money from business news. _____

4   The company is still based on the same ideas. _____

5   The company made good use of information technology throughout its history. _____

Now circle the correct letters A–C.

1   Reuters is best known …
    A   as a financial information service.
    B   as a news agency.
    C   for its wide network of journalists.

2   Paul Reuter moved to London because …
    A   he was near the stock market.
    B   he could supply stock prices over the new Dover–Calais line.
    C   London was important in the telegraphy network.

3   The company expanded when …
    A   the teleprinter was invented.
    B   cables were laid across the continents.
    C   it announced the death of President Lincoln.

4   The company expanded its financial services because …
    A   it introduced Stockmaster.
    B   of increased competition.
    C   of pressure from the British government.

5   Reuters expanded by …
    A   buying other companies.
    B   using satellites to send information.
    C   providing accurate and clear descriptions of events.

Achieve IELTS: **reading for general understanding**

The exam often tests your ability to read quickly and understand the general idea of the passage. One way asks you to match the headings with the paragraphs; another way asks you to match the paragraphs with the descriptions. When you answer a question like this:

1   read the text quickly and underline the key words and sentence(s) that carry the main idea(s) of the paragraph.

2   try to summarise what the paragraph is about.

3   look at the headings or descriptions and decide which are closest to your ideas.

4   reject any headings you think are wrong.

Now underline the main ideas and key words in the passage.

3   Work in pairs. Discuss possible headings for each paragraph.

4   Work in pairs. Discuss the questions.

1   What skills and qualifications do you think you need to work for a press agency?

2   Do you think people should pay for or share information?

Speaking

IELTS tasks: individual long turn – giving longer answers (2)

A

British
corporation
broadcasting
cable
network
Australian
news

1   Write the acronyms in full. Use some of the words in A.

   1 BBC _____   2 CNN _____   3 ABC _____

   Now work in groups. Design a schedule for a college or local radio station. Follow these steps.

   1 Decide who your listeners are and what kind of programmes they would like.

   2 Decide which programmes to broadcast at what time.

   3 Think of a name for your radio station.

2   Work in pairs. Ask each other these questions.

   1 Do you watch or listen to the news often?

   2 What recent events have happened in your country?

   3 Does the media in your country pay more attention to national or worldwide events?

3   Read the topic below and make notes.

Part 2: Describe a recent news story.

You should say:

1   when the event took place

2   where the event took place

3   what happened exactly

and explain why this news story was memorable or important.

   Now answer the questions and expand your notes.

   1 What time of the year was it when the event happened?

   2 Was it important news locally, nationally or internationally?

   3 Where were you when it happened?

   4 In which part of the country did it happen?

   5 How many people were involved?

   6 How did you feel about the event?

   7 How did other people feel about it?

   8 What happened as a result of this?

   9 Why is it memorable or important?

4   Work in pairs. Discuss the topic.

Writing

IELTS tasks: task 1 – giving reasons

1 Work in pairs. Answer the questions.

 1 Where do you usually get news from?
 2 Do you think the Internet is a good source of news?
 3 Where do you think journalists get news from?

2 Match the words with the definitions.

 1 data   a a large amount of information on a computer
 2 database   b numbers that show facts
 3 download   c to take information from the Internet onto your computer
 4 statistics   d facts or information

3 Read the passage and complete the chart.

The chart shows the weekly use of the Internet by journalists in the USA. This is the result of developments in information technology. As the chart shows, the Internet has changed the way journalists work. More than eight in ten say that they use the Internet to keep up with the news. This is because they read news from other organisations or search for press releases. One reason for this is the increased availability of information from these websites. About three-quarters say that at least once a week they communicate via e-mail with readers or listeners. Nearly one-third use the Internet to download raw data from computer databases. Surprisingly, two uses in the survey got a low response: approximately 14 per cent said they interview sources via e-mail. One reason for this is that journalists still prefer face-to-face contact with sources. Only 13 per cent said they use statistical programmes to analyse data.

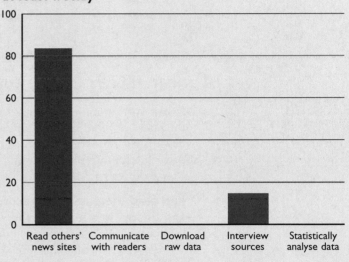

Internet use – percentage of journalists saying *at least weekly*

Source: The American Journalist in the 21st Century

Language study: giving reasons

4 Study the examples and explanation.

> *One reason for this is that journalists still prefer face-to-face contact …*
> *This is the result of developments in information technology …*
> **We use *is + because (of)* / *caused by* / *the result of* to give reasons.**
> *The result of* + (noun phrase) …   *This is because* + (verb clause) …

Now work in pairs. Give reasons for the sentences.

1 News comes from all over the world very quickly.
2 Some people do not trust journalists.
3 In the US, most journalists have degrees.
4 Older people are more critical of news reports.
5 Many broadcasters buy news from agencies.

5 **Look at the table and underline the most important information.**

Now work in pairs. Give reasons for this.

Reasons people give for watching network nightly news less often

Reason/age	18–29	30–49	50+
No time/too busy	64%	50%	21%
Don't have TV	6%	18%	10%
Critical of reporting	2%	8%	31%
No interest in it	9%	7%	15%
Get the same information from other media	5%	10%	15%
Other/don't know/no answer	14%	7%	8%

Source: *The American Journalist in the 21st Century*

Achieve IELTS: giving supporting information

When you write about a chart or table, make sure you include information from the chart or table in your report. Do not include your own opinions about the reasons for the information or compare the information with your country. Always provide accurate information. You can use *about, approximately, nearly, more/less than, around* to refer to numbers and figures in a general way.

Now read the passage in activity 3 again and find ways of referring to numbers and figures in a general way.

---

6 **Write a report for a university lecturer describing the information shown in activity 5. You should write at least 150 words.**

Map A

The map shows Wales with the following locations marked:

Holyhead, Llandudno, Liverpool, Rhyl, Colwyn, Conwy, Bangor, Wrexham, Ffestiniog, Snowdonia National Park, Cumbrian Mountains, Welshpool, Newtown, Aberystwyth, Aberaeron, WALES, Hay-on-Wye, Pembrokeshire Coast National Park, Fishguard, St David's, Brecon Beacons National Park, Laugharne, Pembroke, Merthyr Tydfil, Llanelli, Swansea, Newport, Cardiff, IRISH SEA, ENGLAND

Numbered locations on map: 1 (Bangor area), 2 (Conwy area), 3 (below Conwy), 4 (central Snowdonia), 5 (Swansea area)

1 Caernarfon Castle

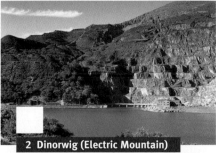

2 Dinorwig (Electric Mountain)

Fieldwork

3 Snowdon

4 National Botanical Gardens of Wales

5 Centre for Alternative Technology

1   Look at map A and decide where you would like to visit.

    Now work in pairs. Compare your answers.

36 2   Listen to a conversation and tick the places you hear.

3 Listen again and complete the notes. Write no more than three words or a number for each answer.

Now circle the correct letter A–C.

> project about (1) _____ development
>
> report (2) _____ words, plus (3) _____
>
> Catherine and Shin are going to (4) _____ Wales
>
> *Thursday*   depart for Snowdon
> *Friday*   Snowdon (5) _____ offices
> *Monday*   Dinorwig hydroelectric (6) _____
> *Tuesday*   Centre for (7) _____ at Machynlleth
> *Thursday*   begin (8) _____

1 Catherine wanted to …
   A do a project during the holiday.
   B go to Spain.
   C go to southwest Wales.

2 The project is …
   A a long essay only.
   B for the second week after the holiday.
   C at the National Botanical Gardens.

3 The Snowdon National Park offices are interesting because …
   A they are beautiful.
   B they do not use a lot of energy.
   C they are built inside a mountain.

Express yourself: free time

 Listen and underline the weak syllables.

he's at a loose end   he wanted to tag along   he's got some time on his hands

Now match the phrases with the definitions.

1 to have some free time
2 to have nothing to do
3 to go with someone

---

4 Match the words in A with the definitions.

A

report
deadline
slide
fieldwork
break
handout

1 research done outside classes
2 a long piece of writing
3 a short holiday
4 an image you show on a screen
5 a paper with information you give to other people
6 the final date for a piece of work

Now match the words in A with these verbs.

set   hand in   take
prepare   show   do

5 Work in pairs. Ask each other the questions.

1 Have you ever done fieldwork?
2 Have you ever written a report?
3 Have you ever missed a deadline?

6 **Work in pairs. Look at the picture and answer the questions.**

1 What do you think it is?

2 How do you think it works?

38 **Now listen to a conversation and complete the notes.**

Opening days
May to October (1) _____
November to March (2) _____
 	
Opening times
May: open (3) _____
       close (4) _____
 	
Tour length (5) _____
	Tour places
	   Visitor centre and
	   (6) _____
	Cost
	Adult £6
	Student (7) _____
	Group rate (20 people)
	   (8) _____

38 **7** **Listen again and circle three letters A–F.**

Which three activities does the tour include?

A tour of the lake
B multi-media sound and vision show
C a presentation

D a film
E a talk
F a tour of the power station

Language study: information questions

8 **Study the examples and explanations.**

> *I wonder if you could give me some information.*
> ***Could you tell me** what Dinorwig is?*
> ***Can you tell me** what the tour includes?*
> ***Would you mind telling me** the group rate?*
>
> **We use information questions when we want to ask for information politely.**
> **Information questions have the same form as statements.**
>
> *What is Dinorwig?* ➤ *Could you tell me **what Dinorwig is**?*
>
> *can/could you + tell (me) + wh- question*
>
> *Would you mind telling me the group rate? **Of course not**; it's £70 per group.*
>
> **We use a negative form to give a positive answer with *would you mind + -ing*.**

Now decide which information question above is the most/least polite.

9 **Work in pairs. Student A, ask for information and complete the notes. Student B, turn to assignment 6.1 and answer the questions.**

EDEN PROJECT

Opening days: _____
Opening times: _____
Cost: Adult _____
      Student _____
Group rate: _____
Tour length: _____

Reading

IELTS tasks: true/false/not given; labelling a diagram

1 **Work in pairs. Look at the picture and try to answer the questions.**

  1 What is it?

  2 Where is it?

    A Turkey   B North America   C South America   D China

  3 How much power does it produce? Enough for …

    A a town.   B a city.   C a region.   D a country.

  4 What topics do you think the reading passage will contain?

    A The advantages of hydropower.

    B How a hydroelectric power station works.

    C Different kinds of hydroelectric power station.

    D Other (what?).

Achieve IELTS: predicting

One way to help you understand a passage is to think about the main ideas before you begin to read it.

1 Read the title and think about what the passage contains.

2 Look at any pictures or diagrams before you read the passage.

Now read the passage and check your answers to question 4.

Hydropower: the fascinating facts

Hydroelectricity is a renewable energy source, since the water flowing in rivers comes from rain or snow. Worldwide, about 24 per cent of the world's electricity is produced by hydropower
5 plants and more than 1 billion people are supplied with power from these plants. Today the largest hydroelectric project in the world is the Itaipu Dam on the border of Brazil and Paraguay, supplying approximately 25 per cent of Brazil's
10 power and 78 per cent of Paraguay's power. However, China's massive Three Gorges Dam will be the largest when it has been completed.

There are six main components to a hydroelectric power station. First, the dam. Most
15 hydropower plants have a dam to contain water, creating a large reservoir of water behind the hydroelectric station. Dams are usually placed where water descends from a height, as the energy that is generated from water depends not
20 only on the volume but also on the difference in height between the dam and the water outflow. This height difference is called the head. For this reason, dams are built as high as possible to produce the maximum electrical energy. However,
25 some early hydroelectric systems used the flow of water over an existing waterfall, with no dam needed; for example, a large amount of electricity is generated by Niagara Falls.

Second, the intake where gates on the dam are
30 opened and water is pulled through the penstock

– a pipe that leads to the turbine. Water pressure is built up as it flows through this pipe. Third, and perhaps the most important component, is the turbine. The turbine has
35 large blades, which are moved by the flow of the water and are attached to a generator above it through a drive shaft. The most
40 common type of turbine for hydropower plants is the Francis Turbine, which looks like a big disc with curved blades.

The Francis Turbine

45 The fourth major component is the generator. As the turbine blades are moved by the water, so are a series of magnets inside the generator. These giant magnets move past copper coils, producing
50 electricity. Fifth, the electric current inside the powerhouse is taken to the transformer and converted to a higher-voltage current. The current is then taken out of the hydroelectric station via power lines. Finally, the water that has
55 been used to generate power is released through an outflow – the water is carried through pipelines and rejoins the river.

An alternative method
60 of hydroelectric power generation is via a pumped storage plant. An example of this is Dinorwig in Wales. This
65 requires two reservoirs: an upper reservoir where water is stored to provide power; and a lower reservoir where water enters from the
70 upper reservoir after being used for power generation. Using a reversible turbine, water is pumped back up to the upper reservoir when the demand for electricity is not as great. The advantage of this kind of hydroelectric power
75 station is that electricity can be generated at times of greatest demand.

2   **Read the passage again. Do the statements agree with the information given in the reading passage?**

Write: TRUE if the statement is true according to the passage.
     FALSE if the statement is false according to the passage.
     NOT GIVEN if the statement is not given in the passage.

1   Hydroelectric power stations supply a large number of people with electricity.   _____

2   Hydroelectric power stations produce some pollution.   _____

3   The amount of electricity produced depends on the amount of water only.   _____

4   Early hydroelectric dams were built on waterfalls.   _____

5   All hydroelectric power stations release water back into a river.   _____

3   **Find words in the reading passage which mean ...**

1   a machine used to generate electricity.

2   an obstacle used to stop water flowing.

3   a large amount of water usually collected by stopping the flow of a river.

4   a machine that moves when water hits it and powers a generator.

5   a device that changes the power of an electric current.

Now read the passage again. Label the diagram using the words in B.

B

reservoir
dam
head
generator
penstock
turbine
outflow
transformer
intake

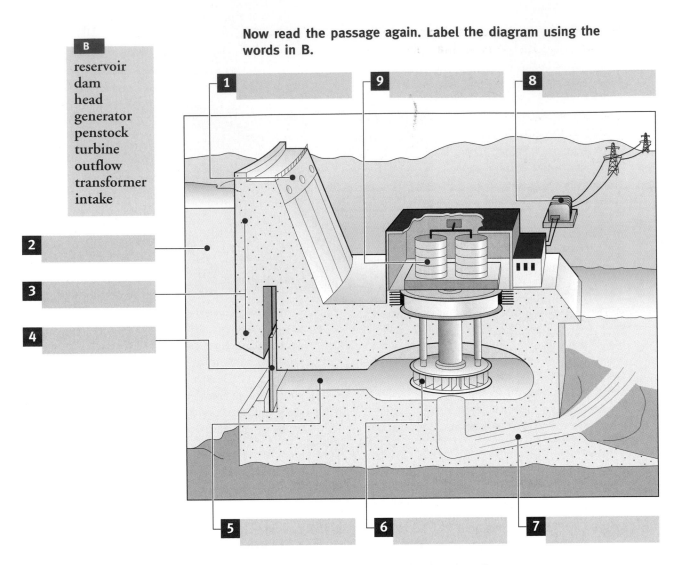

1

2

3

4

5

6

7

8

9

Language study: present passive

4   Study the examples and explanations.

*dams **are built** as high as possible*

*the water that **has been used** to generate power is released*

We use the passive structure to put the important information at the beginning of the sentence. We can use the passive when the subject is obvious, not known or not important.

subject + *be* (*not*) + past participle

*about 24 per cent of the world's electricity is produced **by** hydropower plants*

*energy that is generated **from** water*

We use *by*, *via*, *through* or *from* to include the thing or person that causes the action.

Now look at the diagram and complete the passage with the verbs in brackets.

Fuel cells (1) _____ (use) to power moving vehicles. Many fuel cells (2) _____ (put) together to generate enough energy to move a vehicle. The fuel cells (3) _____ (supply) with hydrogen from the fuel tank and oxygen from outside. As the hydrogen (4) _____ (move) through the cell it touches catalysts which causes it to release electrons. The electrons move through the second catalyst and react with the oxygen. Water (5) _____ (form) and (6) _____ (collect) for reuse.

5 **Work in pairs. Student A turn to assignment 6.2. Describe the diagram to Student B. Student B, label the diagram.**

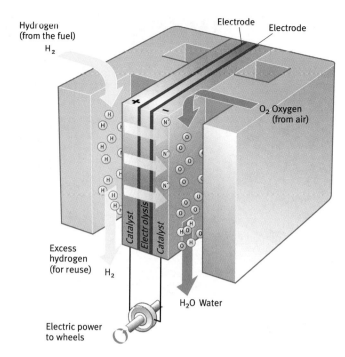

Hydrogen
(from the fuel)
H₂

Electrode   Electrode

O₂ Oxygen
(from air)

Catalyst Electrolysis Catalyst

Excess
hydrogen
(for reuse)   H₂

H₂O Water

Electric power
to wheels

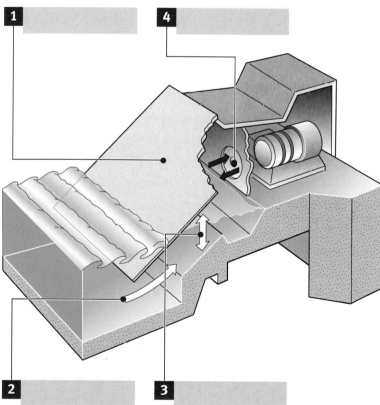

1

4

2

3

Now work in pairs and write a short paragraph about wave power.

Writing

IELTS tasks: describing a process

1   **Work in pairs. Look at the picture and answer the questions.**

1   What do you know about this type of energy production?
2   Does your country use it?
3   How does it work?

2   **Look at the diagram. Complete the description with the words in C.**

C

send
turn
connect
move
increase
take
generate

Wind turbines produce electricity by using the natural power of the wind to drive a generator. A wind turbine is made up of four basic parts: the blades, the shaft, the nacelle and the transformer. First, the blades (1) _____ by the movement of the wind, making them rotate around a hub. As the wind moves, the blades (2) _____ to face the direction of the wind by sensors on the turbine in order to collect the maximum amount of energy. The blades (3) _____ to the nacelle by a shaft. Inside the nacelle are the gearbox and the generator. Electricity (4) _____ as the shaft turns the gearbox. The rotation speed of the shaft (5) _____ by the gearbox. The generator then uses magnets to convert the energy into electricity. When the wind becomes too strong, brakes inside the nacelle can stop the blades. At the next stage, electricity (6) _____ to a transformer nearby. Following this, electricity is transformed to a higher voltage, and finally (7) _____ into the national electricity supply grid.

Now label the diagram. Use the words in D.

D

shaft
gearbox
blade
nacelle
hub

1 _____
2 _____
3 _____
4 _____
5 _____

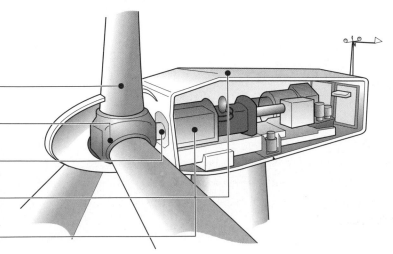

Language study: sequence and purpose

3 **Study the examples and explanation.**

> *First ...*
> *As the wind moves ...*
> *At the next stage ...*
> *The generator* **then** *uses magnets ...*
> *Following this ...*
> *finally ...*
>
> **We use sequencing words and phrases to show the order of events in a process.**
>
> *in order to collect the maximum amount of energy ...*
>
> **We use phrases of purpose to give reasons for the events in a process.**

Now work in pairs. Put the words and phrases in E into groups.

1 sequence:

2 purpose:

4 **Read the passage and answer the questions.**

1 Where does the energy come from when we use biomass?

2 How much energy is produced from biomass in Africa?

3 How many ways of producing biomass energy are included in the passage?

E
after that
in order to
next
so as to
second
the last thing
when
to begin with
so that

Biomass energy: a definition

Biomass is one of the most important and common ways of generating energy. Put simply, it is the production of energy from organic matter. Organic matter that is used as a source of biomass energy includes trees, sugar cane, leaves and manure. According to the World Bank, 50 to 60 per cent of the energy in developing countries of Asia and 70 to 90 per cent of the energy in developing countries in Africa comes from wood or biomass. Biomass is made up mainly of carbon and hydrogen; we use technology to free the energy found in these elements. There are several ways of capturing the stored chemical energy in biomass. The simplest is *direct combustion* – the burning of material by direct heat. *Pyrolysis* is when biomass is heated to a temperature between 400 and 800 degrees C, but no oxygen is introduced, resulting in gas, fuel oil and charcoal. In the tank it is broken down, or digested, into parts, releasing methane gas. In *anaerobic digestion* biomass such as waste water, manure or food waste, is mixed with water and put into a tank without air. In the tank it is broken down, or digested, into parts, releasing methane gas. In *alcohol fermentation*, fuel alcohol is produced by fermenting materials such as wheat, potatoes and waste paper to produce industrial alcohol.

Now read the passage again and find words that mean ...

1 heating something until it burns.

2 the process of burning something at a very high temperature without air.

3 the process of breaking down material into different elements.

4 a chemical process where alcohol is produced from a natural substance.

Biomass energy production

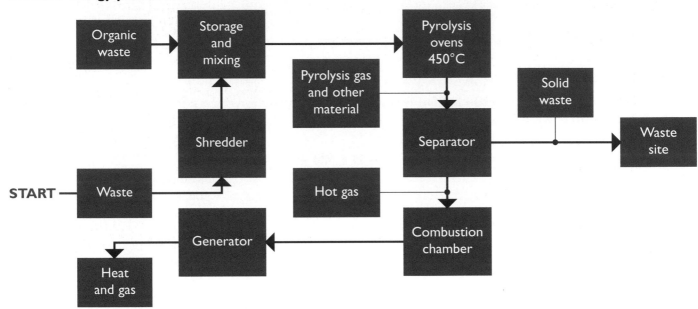

5 **Look at the diagram and order the sentences.**

A Separating the gas and solid materials.

B Heating the oven, without air, to about 450 degrees C.

C Transporting the waste into the pyrolysis oven.

D Producing pyrolysis gas and other solid materials.

E Moving waste to a shredder, after which the waste is taken to a storage pit where it is mixed with more organic waste.   **1**

F Feeding the hot gas into a combustion unit.

G Taking the hot gas to a generator. The generator provides heat and power.

Now write about the diagram using words and phrases for sequencing and purpose and passive sentences.

Listening

IELTS tasks: labelling

1   Look at the picture and answer the questions.

   1   Where do you think it is?

   2   How does it work?

   3   Is this kind of energy used a lot in your country?

39   2   Listen to a talk and match the names with the jobs.

1	Simon	a	professor
2	Karl Micova	b	research assistant
3	Amarina	c	receptionist
4	Sungwoo Jeong	d	administrator

39   Now listen again. Complete the notes and diagram.

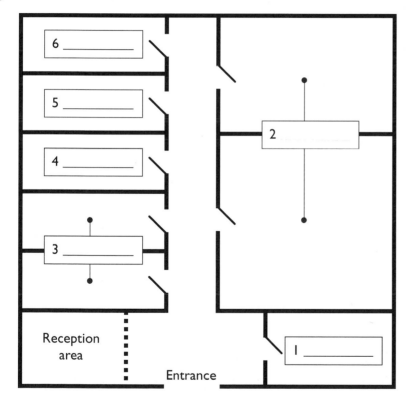

Centre for sustainable energy

part of the Department of
   (1) _____

established (2) _____

(3) _____ staff and
   research students

turnover (4) _____

Amarina will talk about the
   (5) _____

3   Work in pairs. Answer the questions.

   1   Would you like to study at the centre for sustainable energy?

   2   Which type of sustainable energy are you interested in?

4   Read the quiz and choose the answers.

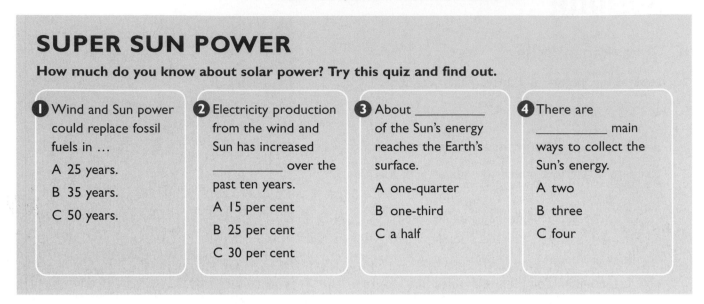

SUPER SUN POWER

How much do you know about solar power? Try this quiz and find out.

1 Wind and Sun power could replace fossil fuels in …

A 25 years.

B 35 years.

C 50 years.

2 Electricity production from the wind and Sun has increased _____ over the past ten years.

A 15 per cent

B 25 per cent

C 30 per cent

3 About _____ of the Sun's energy reaches the Earth's surface.

A one-quarter

B one-third

C a half

4 There are _____ main ways to collect the Sun's energy.

A two

B three

C four

40   Now listen to a lecture and check your answers.

40 **5**   Listen again and label the diagram.

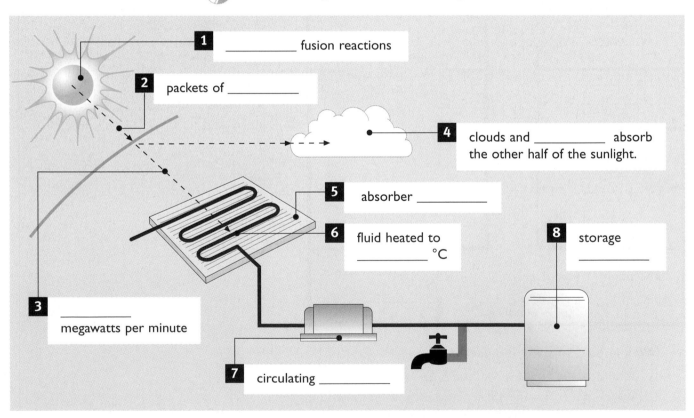

1 _____ fusion reactions

2 packets of _____

4 clouds and _____ absorb the other half of the sunlight.

5 absorber _____

6 fluid heated to _____ °C

8 storage _____

3 _____ megawatts per minute

7 circulating _____

Now work in pairs and discuss the questions.

1 Which information in the lecture did you find interesting or surprising?

2 What are the advantages of solar power?

3 Are there any disadvantages?

Speaking

IELTS tasks: individual long turn – rounding-off questions (2)

1 **Work in pairs. Decide which energy sources are sustainable.**

- [ ] hydroelectric
- [ ] solar
- [ ] nuclear
- [ ] coal
- [ ] geothermal
- [ ] gas
- [ ] wave
- [ ] oil
- [ ] wind

2 **Read the text and tick the things you do.**

ENERGY AND BUILDINGS

- [ ] Turn off lights you aren't using – including those things with LCDs, like video recorders.
- [ ] Make sure your heating is efficient, and turn it down when you can.
- [ ] Consider solar heating. Decide if a solar water heating system will work in your house – it can pay you back in two or three years.

GETTING THERE

- [ ] Use public transport rather than private.
- [ ] Cut out unnecessary journeys, share cars, use public transport and, if you can, live near your work or school, or work from home.
- [ ] Use your bicycle as much as you can.
- [ ] Avoid going by plane; it is by far the most polluting way of travel.

SHOPPING

- [ ] Buy things that don't use unnecessary packaging.
- [ ] Buy local food and drink. Think of all the energy used to transport produce from distant countries.

Now work in pairs. Compare your answers.

3 **Read the topic and make notes.**

> **Part 2: Describe ways in which you save energy.**
> *You should say:*
> *1 what you do*
> *2 how it helps*
> *3 how long you have done this for*
> *and explain why it is important to do these things.*

Now tick the rounding-off questions for the topic.

- [ ] Does your country have any solar power stations?
- [ ] How do you encourage other people to save energy?
- [ ] How does your country generate electricity?
- [ ] How many national parks are in your country?

4 **Work in pairs. Ask each other about the topic and the relevant rounding-off questions.**

UNIT 7
Cities

Cosmopolitan

1 **Work in pairs. Ask each other the questions.**

1 Do you like where you live?
2 Would you like to live in another place?
3 Where wouldn't you like to live?

2 **Match the opposite words.**

overcrowded	new	noisy	clean
quiet	dirty	spacious	horrible
inland	large	dynamic	old
pleasant	small	boring	coastal

Now work in pairs. Describe your home town/city.

41 **3** **Listen to a conversation and tick the words in 2 you hear.**

41 Now listen again and complete notes A. Write no more than three words and/or a number for each answer.

Tokyo
1 location:
2 founded:
3 population:
4 area (m²):
5 number of universities:

Express yourself: talking about cities

42 Listen and complete the sentences.

1 So _____ are you from?
2 I _____ Tokyo is a very old city.
3 I _____ it was always the capital city.
4 _____ Tokyo a coastal city ...

42 Now listen again and practise.

Language study: comparatives

4 **Study the examples and explanations.**

> *it's **older than** Sydney*
>
> **When we compare two or more things we use adjective + -er (than) for words with one or two syllables.**
>
> *in many ways it's **more attractive than** Tokyo*
>
> **We use more + adjective (than) for words with more than two syllables. Some two-syllable words follow this pattern.**
>
> *Our metro system is **better than** here ...*
>
> **Some adjectives are irregular.**
>
> *it's **much less** crowded here than back home*
>
> **We use (much) more/less + adjective (than) to compare quantities.**
>
> *So is it **as hot as** Sydney?*
>
> **We use as + adjective + as to say something is similar.**

Now work in pairs. Decide how to form the comparative adjectives of the words in B.

5 **Write three sentences comparing your home town with Sydney or Tokyo.**

6 **Work in pairs. Discuss these questions.**

1 Have you been to either Sydney or London?
2 Which would you like to go to?

Now read the passage on the following page and complete the chart for Sydney.

B

beautiful
cold
pleasant
humid
bad

A

Sydney
location: _____
founded: _____
population: _____
area (m²): _____
number of universities: _____

B

London
location: *south-east of England*
founded: *AD 50*
population: *over 7 million*
area (m²): *1,500 km²*
number of universities: *12*

SYDNEY

From its beginnings just 200 years ago Sydney has grown to become one of the world's great cities. It is often said to be one of the most beautiful and liveable cities in the world. Sydney is a coastal city in the south-east of Australia. Its main features are the magnificent Sydney harbour and its shoreline, which extends for over 300 kilometres. At the farthest ends of the coast are national parks. The city centre is on the southern side of the harbour, just inland from the harbour. On the northern side of the harbour are the affluent northern suburbs. The southern and northern sides of the city are linked by Sydney Harbour bridge.

Australians are well known for their love of sport and in 2000 Sydney hosted the Olympic games; the Olympic park is west of the city. Sydney has five universities, making it very student-friendly. Although it has 20 per cent of Australia's total population (3.7 million people), Sydney is not at all overcrowded because it is the world's largest city in area at 5,000 square kilometres in size – twice the size of Beijing and six times the size of London. In fact, it can take half a day just to get to a destination, so plan your sightseeing carefully.

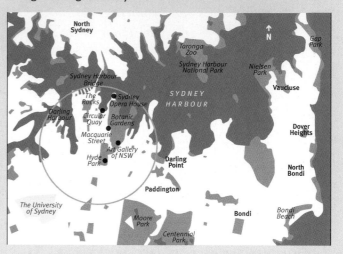

7   Answer the questions.

1   What are Sydney's main geographical features?
2   What are Australians well known for?
3   Why should you plan your sightseeing carefully?
4   Does anything surprise you about the city?

Language study: superlatives

8   Study the examples and explanations.

> *it is the world's largest city in area*
> **When we compare more than two things we use *the* + adjective + *est* for adjectives with one or two syllables.**
>
> *one of the most beautiful and liveable cities in the world*
> **With adjectives with more than two syllables we use *the most* + adjective.**
>
> *At the farthest ends of the coast are national parks.*
> **Some adjectives are irregular – for example *good*, *bad* and *far*.**

Now answer the questions about London, Tokyo and Sydney.
1   Which is the oldest city?
2   Which city has the largest population?
3   Which city has the most universities?
4   Which city has the largest area?

9   Work in pairs. Compare three cities in your country.

Speaking

IELTS tasks: individual long turn – describing cities

1 Label the pictures with these cities.

Rio de Janeiro   Edinburgh   Singapore   Bangkok   Istanbul

1 Now listen to a talk and decide which city the speaker talks about.

2 Listen again and number the subjects in the order you hear them.

☐ geography   ☐ location   ☐ opinion
☐ description   ☐ history

Pronunciation

2 3 Listen and notice how the voice rises and falls.

Europe and Asia
the Bosphorous on one side and the Black Sea on the other
founded by the Greeks and developed by the Romans

2 Now listen again and practise.

4 Work in pairs. Student A, turn to assignment 7.1 and describe the city. Student B, decide which city Student A describes.

Now Student B, turn to assignment 7.2 and describe the city. Student A, decide which city Student B describes.

5 Read the topic and make notes.

> **Part 2: Describe a city you know well.**
> *You should say:*
> 1   *where it is*
> 2   *what it is like*
> 3   *what special places or features it has*
> *and explain why you like or dislike it.*

Now tick the rounding-off questions for the topic.

☐ How long have you lived there?
☐ Is it as nice as Paris?
☐ Have you got any special memories about it?
☐ What other cities would you like to visit?

6 Work in pairs. Student A, you are the examiner; interview Student B. Student B, you are the candidate; answer the questions.

A

B

C

D

E

Reading

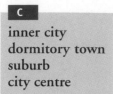

C

inner city
dormitory town
suburb
city centre

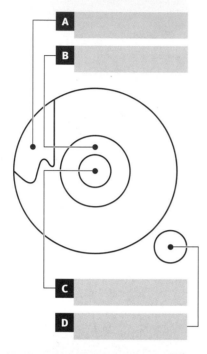

IELTS tasks: matching headings and paragraphs; table completion; true/false/not given

1   Label the diagram. Use the words in C.

   Now work in pairs. Say where you live.

2   Read the passage and choose the most suitable headings for sections A–E from the list of headings.

> **List of headings**
> i   Megacities around the world
> ii   The formation of megacities
> iii What is a megacity?
> iv   Megacities and the individual
> v   Problems megacities share
> vi   Megacities in developing countries
> vii Cities lose their people

1 Section A _____   4 Section D _____
2 Section B _____   5 Section E _____
3 Section C _____

Megacities: a new kind of city

A The term 'megalopolis' (or megacity) was first used by French geographer Jean Gottman to describe the north-eastern United States in 1961. The term is used more widely now and is defined as an urban area of more than 10 million inhabitants dominated by low-density housing. In 1995 there were 14 megacities. By 2015 there could be 21.

B Megacities are the result of the process of urbanisation. After cities grew into crowded urban centres, people who could afford to moved into suburbs at the edge of the city. When the suburbs in turn became crowded, people moved into villages and dormitory towns outside the city, but within commuting distance. In this way, for the first time since industrialisation, the countryside began to gain population, whereas cities lost their inhabitants. In the 1980s St Louis and Detroit in America lost between 35 and 47 per cent of their populations and London lost 15 per cent in the 20 years to 1971.

C However, this movement away from cities does not mean that the city is dying. In fact it is spreading. From the old city develops a metropolitan area with many low-level urban developments. When these metropolitan areas merge together, they form megacities which contain over 10 million people. The largest of these is in America, called Boswash – a region over 300 miles long from Boston in the north to Washington DC in the south with more than 44 million people. There are emerging megalopolises in Britain centred around London and the south-east, in Germany in the industrial region of the Ruhr and in Japan in the Tokyo-Osaka-Kyoto region.

D Megacities used to be concentrated in the developed regions but today the greater number are in developing countries – mainly in East and South Asia. Today the five largest cities are Tokyo, Mexico City, Sao Paulo, New York City and Mumbai. In 2015 they will probably be Tokyo, Dhaka, Mumbai, Sao Paulo and Delhi. At the moment just under 394 million people live in megacities, 246 million in developing countries. In 2015 there will be about 600 million people living in megacities and by 2030 60 per cent of the world's people will be living in megacities.

E Megacities have a number of similar specific problems. Among common problems are high population concentration, high traffic levels, housing problems and, in some cases, extreme socio-economic differences. However, large population numbers alone do not create these problems; city problems are thought to be caused mostly by weak and unrepresentative city governments.

Now read sections B and C again and complete the table. Use no more than three words for each point.

Change	Result
city centres become crowded	(1) people _____
suburbs become crowded	(2) people _____
(3) _____	many low-level urban developments
(4) _____	a megacity is formed

3 **Read the passage again. Do the statements reflect the claims of the writer?**

Write: TRUE if the statement is true according to the passage.
FALSE if the statement is false according to the passage.
NOT GIVEN if the statement is not given in the passage.

1 A megacity is characterised by high-rise apartment blocks. _____

2 Cities lose their populations when poorer people move into them. _____

3 Movement away from cities creates metropolitan areas. _____

4 There will be more megacities in developed countries than in developing countries. _____

5 Problems in very large cities are mostly due to poor administration. _____

4 **Work in pairs. Discuss the questions.**

1 Do you live in a megacity?
2 Would you like to live in a megacity?
3 Do you think there are any advantages to living in a megacity?

A

B

C

D

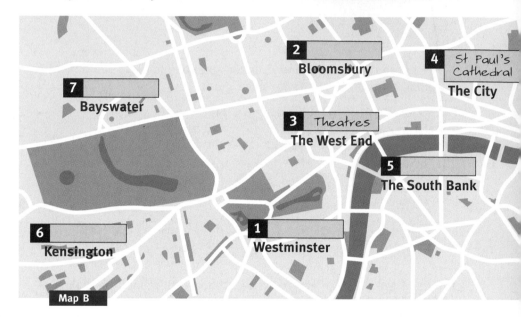

E

Listening

IELTS tasks: labelling; note completion; table completion

1 Match the places in D with the pictures.

2 Listen to a conversation and label map B with the places in 1.

2 Bloomsbury

4 St Paul's Cathedral
The City

7 Bayswater

3 Theatres
The West End

5
The South Bank

6 Kensington

1 Westminster

Map B

3 Listen again and complete the notes with no more than two words for each answer.

Westminster: Parliament and other (1) _____ are here.
South Bank: a centre for the (2) _____ with galleries and theatres.
West End: you can see a (3) _____ here.
The City: the (4) _____ district of London.
Bloomsbury: just (5) _____ of the City.
Kensington: a well-off, (6) _____ part of London.

4 Work in pairs. Discuss which places in London you would like to visit and why.

5   **Read the notes and decide whether each answer is a number or other information.**

Garden suburbs started in Britain, but during the (1) _____ centuries developed in Australia. By the 1890s (2) _____ of Sydney's population lived in suburbs.

In the USA suburbs have low populations, but have no (3) _____. In the 1990s suburbs grew more quickly than (4) _____ in the US.

(5) _____ of suburban expansion in the West is being done in 20 years in Southeast Asia. People prefer (6) _____ so the population is high and development speed is quick. One town in Korea grew from nothing to (7) _____ people in five years. In Asian cities (8) _____ is already a problem because people have to use (9) _____ and buses.

Scientists measure suburbs using the 'sprawl index'. A high sprawl index points to an (10) _____.

Now work in pairs. Discuss the possible answers.

6   **Listen to a lecture and complete the notes in 5. Write no more than three words and/or a number for each answer.**

7   **Complete the chart with Southeast Asia (SA) or America/Australia (A/A).**

Country	Problem
1 _____	traffic congestion
2 _____	overweight people
3 _____	high population density
4 _____	traffic deaths
5 _____	pollution

Now work in pairs. Discuss the questions.

1   Are suburbs in your country similar to those in Australia or South Korea?
2   Do suburbs in your county have similar problems to those in America and Australia?

Writing

IELTS tasks: task 1 – comparing and contrasting changes

1   Work in pairs. Ask each other the questions.

1   What is the population of your city?   2   Is your city expanding?

Now look at the chart and answer the questions.

1   What does the chart show?
2   Can you put the information into groups?
3   Does any of the information surprise you?
4   Can you think of any reasons for the changes?

2   Put the sentences into two groups.

1   comparing/contrasting: 2   classifying:

1   In comparison with New York, Tokyo's population has a much higher rate of increase.
2   We can divide the cities into two main groups.
3   When we compare London and Paris we can see they have similar population sizes.
4   New York's population is growing steadily; on the other hand Dhaka is growing very rapidly.
5   In contrast with cities like Mumbai, Mexico City and Sao Paulo, London is losing its population.
6   We can also make a distinction between cities in developed and developing nations.

Now underline the words and phrases for comparing, contrasting and classifying.

City populations 1950–2015

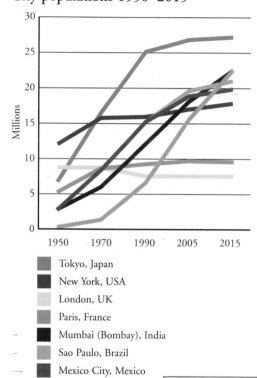

■ Tokyo, Japan
■ New York, USA
■ London, UK
■ Paris, France
■ Mumbai (Bombay), India
■ Sao Paulo, Brazil
■ Mexico City, Mexico
■ Dhaka, Bangladesh

Achieve IELTS: comparing graphs

Candidates who analyse and compare information given in a graph may score higher marks than candidates who just describe the information.

When you write about a graph ask yourself these questions.

1   Can I see any similar information and can I put this in groups?
2   Can I compare and contrast the information?
3   Which words and phrases for comparing and contrasting can I use?

---

3   Underline the key words in the essay title and make notes.

> The chart shows the rate of growth of eight cities in developing and industrialised countries between 1950 and 2015. Write a report for a university lecturer describing the information in the chart.
>
> Now write a 150 word report.

UNIT 8
Communication

In touch

1 Work in pairs. Discuss the questions.

1 How many new developments in communications can you think of?

2 Have new communication technologies made our lives better or worse?

2 Work in pairs. Look at picture A and discuss what has happened.

Now listen to a conversation and check your answers.

3 Listen again and complete the bill.

Now circle the correct letter A–C.

1 Sara uses her mobile phone …
   A very often.
   B often.
   C not very often.

2 Someone rang and …
   A left a message.
   B left a number to call.
   C Sara was rude to them.

3 Sara phoned …
   A and heard a long message.
   B a premium line service.
   C the same number three times.

A

TURQUOISE
MOBILE COMMUNICATIONS

Phone bill		
Total cost of calls	(1) _____	
Items		
(2) _____	£30.00	
Dialled numbers		
Minutes of free calls	(3) _____	
07776 281 443	(4) _____	
(5) _____	£19.20	
090 33 66 55	(6) _____	(x 2)

Express yourself: disbelief

Tick the expressions of disbelief.

- [ ] What's up?
- [ ] I don't believe it.
- [ ] … that can't be right.
- [ ] Never mind.
- [ ] No way!
- [ ] … there must be a mistake.

Now listen and practise.

A

SIM card	keypad	charger
hash key	receiver	menu
star key	screen	battery

1

2

3

4

5

6

7

8

9

4 **Work in pairs. Choose a situation and write a conversation.**

1 You have received a very expensive electricity bill.

2 Your new computer broke down the day after it arrived.

3 A lot of money has gone from your bank account.

Now practise the conversation.

5 **Label the picture. Use the words in A.**

6 **Listen to a message and write the key next to the options.**

> 1, 2, 3, 4, 5, 6, *, #

A to return to the menu _____

B to join from another network _____

C other enquiries _____ , _____

D information about premium line charges _____

E to upgrade your phone _____

F to talk to someone _____

G information about your recent order _____

H join the network _____

I more information about the advertisements _____

J to hear the options again _____

Language study: real conditionals

7 **Study the examples and explanations.**

> *If you **want** to talk to someone, please press 3.*
>
> *If you **are calling** about our latest adverts and **want** more information, press 1.*
>
> *Please **press** 4 if you **want** us to send you information …*
>
> *If* + present (continuous) + verb
>
> **We use real conditionals to talk about the certain result of an action. We often use it to talk about causes and effects, and we often use the structure to give instructions or say how something works. We can replace *if* with *when* or *as soon as*.**
>
> **We use *if* for something that may happen, we use *when/as soon as* for something we are sure will happen. We can change the order of the two parts of the sentence.**

Now write an answerphone message for your school or another organisation.

8 **Work in pairs. Ask each other these questions.**

1 Do you have a mobile phone?

2 Do you use your mobile phone often?

3 When do you use your phone? *I use my phone if I'm late for a meeting or a date.*

Reading

IELTS tasks: labelling; classification

1 Match the words in B with the definitions.

1 to stop someone getting access to something
2 a way of getting money dishonestly
3 something you get for being successful in a competition
4 a piece of paper you can use instead of money
5 to charge more money than the product should be
6 when something is more expensive than it should be

Now read the passage and find two scams and three ways to avoid them.

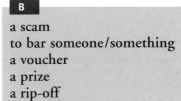

B

a scam
to bar someone/something
a voucher
a prize
a rip-off
to overcharge

AVOIDING PHONE SCAMS

Having a mobile phone brings personal freedom, but this also means freedom to make mistakes. Watch out for these new telephone scams:

A special computer rings your phone number for just one ring, leaving a missed call message and a number to ring back. When you ring the number, you get a long answerphone message or someone trying to keep you talking. Meanwhile, the company is overcharging you – you could be paying as much as £20 a minute for the call. Another rip-off is a text message which says you have won a fantastic prize, but as soon as you call to collect your prize, they send you a voucher and a large bill for calling.

Protect yourself. Follow this advice.

- If the number begins with 090, it's probably a premium rate line.
- Unless you are over 18, do not call a premium rate line number without permission.
- When you get an unwanted call, ask the network to bar that number in case they call again.
- If the source of the prize is overseas, beware of a scam.
- When there is a short time to claim your prize, think twice about calling.
- If you are asked to buy something before you get the prize, or if they ask for bank or credit card details, don't buy the item and never give them the information.
- Do not ring a missed call unless you already know the number.

Language study: *unless, in case*

2 Study the examples and explanation.

Unless you are over 18, do not call a premium line number without permission.
*Do not ring a missed call **unless** you already know the number.*
*... ask the network to bar that number **in case** they call again.*

We use *unless* to say *if ... not*. We use *in case* to say how to avoid a problem in the future.

Now complete the conversation. Use *unless*, *if*, *in case* or *when*.

Sara: Hello. I'm calling about my recent mobile phone bill. I was overcharged for two calls I made.

Customer service advisor: Which calls do you mean exactly?

Sara: (1) _____ you look at the two calls made on 5 May, you can see I was charged at a premium rate.

Customer service advisor: I'm afraid there's not much we can do (2) _____ you called the number, (3) _____ you can show us that the call was made without your agreement.

Sara: No, but they didn't say how much the call cost.

Customer service advisor: (4) _____ you ring a missed number, you must make sure who you're calling. (5) _____ you call, you're entering into an agreement with the company. Would you like us to bar that number (6) _____ they try it again?

Sara: Well, if there's nothing else you can do …

3 **Listen to the conversation and check your answers.**

Now work in pairs. Practise the conversation.

4 **Work in pairs. Circle the correct letter A or B.**

1 Mobile phones are more popular in …
   A America.   B Europe.

2 The world's biggest mobile phone maker is in …
   A Japan.   B Finland.

3 In Britain it is …
   A legal   B illegal
   to use your mobile phone in a traffic jam.

5 **Label the diagram. Use the words in C.**

6 **Read the passage and order pictures A–C.**

1

2

3

4

C

handset
cell
frequency
cable

Mobile communication: back to basics

Many people think that mobile phones are a recent invention. However, they have been available since the mid-1980s and the technology dates back to the 19th century. We can trace the origin of mobile phone technology to Alexander Bell (telephony), and Nikolai Tesla and Gugliemo Marconi (radio). Mobile phones are actually small radios.

Mobile communication is made possible through three basic items: a mobile phone (or handset), switching centres and base stations. An area is broken into a series of hexagonal cells; the cells may be only 500 metres apart in cities or 10 kilometres apart in the countryside. Each hexagon contains a base station, which communicates with the handset; the nearer you are to a base station, the clearer the signal. Base stations are linked to the telephone network through cables and to other base stations. The base stations are controlled by switching centres. Switching centres are, in fact, sophisticated computers called *mobile telephone switching offices* which monitor all mobile phone calls, track the location of the handsets in their area and keep billing information. When the user moves between cells the switching centres pass the handset's signal from base station to base station.

In order to do this, every mobile phone has two channels: a duplex channel through which people can talk and listen at the same time, and a control channel. The duplex channel is really two frequencies: one to talk over and one to listen over. When a mobile phone is switched on, it looks for the control channel of the nearest base station. Through this channel the base station transmits its system identification code – a five-digit number that shows the network provider. If the handset cannot find any control channels, it displays a *no signal* message. When the phone finds a control channel, it also sends a registration request to the switching centre. In this way the switching centre knows where the handset is. If the switching centre receives a call for a user, first it tries to find the handset, then it chooses a frequency pair for the handsets to use. Next, it communicates with the handsets through the control channel and tells them which frequencies to use. Once your handset and the base station are set to those frequencies, the call is connected.

The switching centre also monitors the strength of the signal through the base station. When the base station sees the handset's signal strength decreasing it tells the switching centre. At the same time the next base station sees the handset's signal increasing and also tells the switching centre. At this point the handset gets a signal through the control channel telling it to change to the new frequencies provided by the new base station, and the call continues.

Now label the pictures.

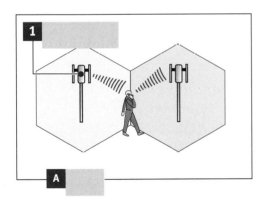

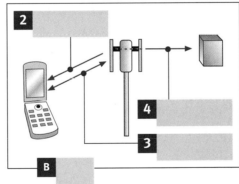

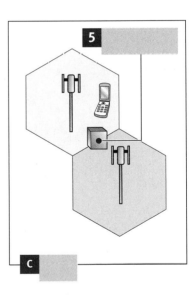

7   **Read the passage again. Complete the sentences with *handset,* *base station* or *switching centre*.**

1   The _____ are located within the cells.

2   _____ control base stations.

3   Mobile phone calls are monitored by _____ .

4   A *no signal* message is displayed by the _____ if it cannot find a control channel.

5   The _____ tells the switching centre when a signal is getting weaker.

8   **Work in pairs. Ask each other the questions.**

1   Which information in the reading passage did you find surprising or interesting?

2   Do you live near a base station?

3   Do you have concerns about radio waves from mobile phones?

mobile phone
flash drive
digital recorder
MP3 player
palmtop

Speaking

IELTS tasks: individual long turn – descriptions (1)

1   Label the pictures with the words in D.

1   2   3   4   5

Now work in pairs. Talk about an item or piece of equipment you would like to have.

2   Read the topic below and make notes.

> **Part 2: Describe an electronic item which is very important to you.**
> *You should say:*
> *1 what it looks like   2 what it does   3 how it works   4 how long you have had it*
> *and explain why it is important to you.*

 Now listen to people talking and decide what items in activity 1 are described.

 3   Listen again and complete the table.

	1	2
size/weight		
material		
colour	—	
other features		

Pronunciation

4   Read the phrases and mark the stressed words.

this is very handy   *the best thing about it is*
I carry this everywhere with me   *I definitely couldn't live without it*

10 Now listen and practise.

5   Work in pairs. Discuss the topic in 2.

6   Read the topic and example questions below. Underline the key words.

> **Part 3: Let's consider the usefulness of electronic items.**
> *1 Which electronic items are popular in your country?*
> *2 Do new electronic items make our lives more complicated or more convenient?*

Now make notes for your answer.

7   Work in groups. Ask each other the questions and discuss the topic.

Listening

IELTS tasks: note completion

1 **Match the words with the definitions.**

1	concern	a	something to stop a dangerous situation
2	evidence	b	the possibility of something bad happening
3	issue	c	a fact or situation that makes people worried
4	precaution	d	an important subject that people are discussing
5	risk	e	facts and information that show something is true

2 **Read the title of the lecture and decide what things will be included.**

11/12 **Now listen to the lecture and check your answers.**

11 **3** **Listen to part 1 again. Complete the notes for the first part of the lecture only. Write no more than three words or a number for each answer.**

> The effect of mobile phones on human health
>
> Part 1
>   Two-thirds of people in the UK own a mobile phone
> and ¼ think their mobile phone is an (1) _____
> of their lives. This lecture is about the (2) _____
>   _____ of mobile phones on humans. The main
> concerns are about (3) _____ used to send radio
> waves to and from the network. People working
> with powerful radio waves said they couldn't (4)
>   _____ . We do not have enough knowledge to say
> mobile phones are (5) _____ .

Now answer the questions.

1 How much does the average person spend on their mobile phone each year?
2 When did scientists discover the effects of radio waves?
3 Who set up an enquiry?

4 **Listen to part 2 again. Complete the notes for the second part of the lecture. Write no more than three words and/or a number for each answer.**

Part 2

Mobile phones heat up (1) _____ ; after making long calls people complain of fatigue (2) _____ headaches and loss of concentration; mobile phone users are (3) _____ times more likely to get cancer next to the ear; there is a link between (4) _____ and cancer in children. Future research: the effect of radio waves on our ability to concentrate (5) _____ ; the connection between mobile phone use and (6) _____ ; long-term effect on people who have used mobiles since (7) _____ .

Now work in pairs. The lecture gives contrasting reasons for 1–4 – what are these?

mobile phones heat up the skin x *not powerful enough to damage people*

5 **Work in pairs. Student A, make a list of advantages of using mobile phones. Student B, make a list of disadvantages of using mobile phones. Try to give examples to support your points.**

Now discuss the advantages and disadvantages of mobile phones.

Writing

IELTS tasks: discursive essay – preparation

1 **Do the quiz.**

> ## Writing: the right way
>
> **Are you careful? Or does your pen have a mind of its own? Try this quick quiz to find out.**
>
> | When I write something I ... | never | usually | always |
> | --- | --- | --- | --- |
> | **1** spend a long time thinking about what to write. | 1 | 2 | 3 |
> | **2** can write quickly. | 1 | 2 | 3 |
> | **3** read what I have written. | 1 | 2 | 3 |
> | **4** look for any mistakes in my writing. | 1 | 2 | 3 |
> | **5** try to remember my mistakes and not repeat them. | 1 | 2 | 3 |

Now turn to assignment 8.1 and read your results.

2 **Read the writing task below and decide if the statements are true or false.**

> You should spend about 40 minutes on this task. Present a written argument or case to an educated reader with no specialist knowledge of the following topic.
>
> *Advances in mobile communication technology have been one of the most important developments in the late 20th century. To what extent do you agree or disagree with this statement?*
>
> You should use your own ideas, knowledge and experience, and support your arguments with examples and relevant evidence. You should write at least 250 words.

1 You have three-quarters of an hour for this task.
2 You are writing for someone with no knowledge of the subject.
3 You are expected to support your ideas and arguments with your own experiences.
4 There is no problem if you write 150 words.

3 **Order the stages of writing an essay from the first thing to the last.**

☐ Write the essay. (____ minutes)
☐ Read the essay again for mistakes and correct the mistakes. (____ minutes)
☐ Make a list of ideas; decide which are relevant and reject irrelevant ideas. (____ minutes)
☐ Read the title and underline the key words. (____ minutes)
☐ Break your ideas into sections and make a plan. (____ minutes)
☐ Read the essay for sense. (____ minutes)

Now decide how many minutes to spend on each stage.

Achieve IELTS: timing and length

It is important to keep to the time and length limits of the test. At the end of the exam you will be told to put down your pens and you should not try to keep writing.

- Remember you have 40 minutes to plan and write the essay.
- Practise listing ideas for the essay title within 10 minutes.
- Practise writing 250 words within 30 minutes.
- Time yourself and see if your writing speed improves.
- Take a watch into the exam.

4 **Read the title of the writing task in activity 2 again and underline the key words.**

5 **Read the list of ideas for the writing task in 2. Decide which are relevant (R), which are irrelevant (I) and which are partially relevant (PR).**

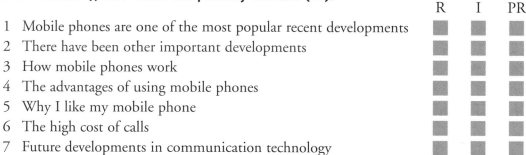

	R	I	PR
1 Mobile phones are one of the most popular recent developments	▪	▪	▪
2 There have been other important developments	▪	▪	▪
3 How mobile phones work	▪	▪	▪
4 The advantages of using mobile phones	▪	▪	▪
5 Why I like my mobile phone	▪	▪	▪
6 The high cost of calls	▪	▪	▪
7 Future developments in communication technology	▪	▪	▪

Now work in pairs. Think of examples and ideas to support the relevant points.

6 **Work in pairs. Read the writing task below and ...**

1 underline the key words.
2 make a list of ideas.
3 think of examples to support your ideas.
4 break your ideas into sections and make an essay plan.

Mobile phones have many benefits, but the effects of mobile phones on human health mean the dangers are greater than the benefits. To what extent do you agree or disagree with this statement?

Get fit!

1   **Label the picture. Choose from the words in A.**

   Now work in pairs. Say which sports you have tried.

13 2   **Listen to the conversation and tick the sports you hear.**

13   **Now listen again. Complete the sentences with no more than three words or a number for each answer.**

Paul has nearly finished (1) _____ of the computer game. Lily is concerned that Paul is putting (2) _____ . Lily wants to (3) _____ something . Kendo is a sport from (4) _____ . There is a (5) _____ for beginners in the evening. They will need to wear (6) _____ . They can catch the (7) _____ bus to the Sturt gymnasium.

3   **Answer the questions.**

   1   What happened when Paul tried windsurfing?
   2   What does Paul say about playing rugby?
   3   How do you score points in Kendo?

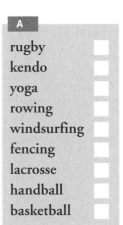

A	
rugby	☐
kendo	☐
yoga	☐
rowing	☐
windsurfing	☐
fencing	☐
lacrosse	☐
handball	☐
basketball	☐

Express yourself: talking about ability

14   **Listen and practise the expressions.**

   I'm really good at this game.   *I'm quite good with a sword.*
   ... I'm not good at sailing.   *... I'm no good at sports.*
   ... there must be some sports you haven't had a go at.
   I'm useless at most of them.   *I fancy having a try at that ...*

   Now match the two parts of the sentences.

   1   I'm no good at   a   water.
   2   I'm very good with   b   sailing.
   3   I'm useless in   c   a racket.

4 **Work in pairs. Ask each other these questions.**

1 Which sport would you like to try?   2 Why haven't you tried it yet?

3 Do you know anyone else who has tried this sport?

5 **Work in pairs. Read the title of the passage below and discuss what a blue is.**

LOCAL GIRL WINS SPORTING BLUE

University student Carol Stanhope has been awarded a blue for her performance in the handball team. She is a third year business student at the University of Darwin, and hopes to be included in the Olympic team in 2008. She has already represented her country several times overseas, including at the World Cup in Denmark.

She trains after classes on week nights, and on Saturdays. On Sundays she plays in a league game – and she is also a full-time student. Being awarded a blue means that her performance is outstanding at an international level. Says Miss Stanhope, 'This recognition means a lot to me. I am looking forward to the Olympics, and hope to win a medal for my country.'

Now read the passage and answer the questions.

1 What sport does Carol play?

2 What does she study?

3 Has she played in other countries?

4 How many days a week does she train?

5 What does she want to do?

15 **6** **Listen to an interview and circle A–D.**

1 Dr Rees attended Cambridge in …
   A the 1920s.
   B the 1930s.
   C the 1940s.
   D the 1950s.

2 She won blues for …
   A swimming and chess.
   B athletics.
   C lacrosse and swimming.
   D rowing and cricket.

3 Lacrosse comes from …
   A South America.
   B Canada.
   C India.
   D France.

4 *The Tadpoles* is a …
   A club for swimming blues.
   B club for lacrosse blues.
   C restaurant in Cambridge.
   D sports stadium.

15 **Now listen again and complete each sentence with no more than three words.**

Blues are awarded to students who (1) _____ in sport. Senior sports such as swimming and athletics are awarded with a (2) _____ blue, whereas minor sports like lacrosse get a (3) _____ blue. Students who win a blue are allowed to wear a (4) _____ and a (5) _____ or a (6) _____ .

7 **Work in pairs. Discuss the questions.**

1 Do you have *blues* at universities in your country?

2 What is your national sport?

3 What sports are your country good at?

Listening

IELTS tasks: note completion; matching

1   Label the picture. Use the words in B.

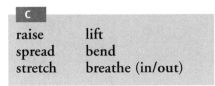

B		
stomach	neck	back
hand	leg	shoulder
chest	hips	elbow
arm	spine	bottom

Now match the words in C with the definitions.

C	
raise	lift
spread	bend
stretch	breathe (in/out)

1   move one end toward the other
2   move apart
3   to put something in a higher position
4   to make part of your body as straight as possible
5   to carry something to a higher position
6   make air go in or out of your chest

16   2   Listen to a yoga instructor and complete the notes with no more than three words for each answer.

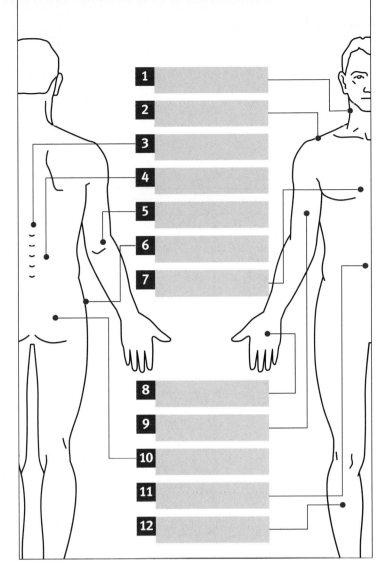

Sitting position Sit cross-legged with your hands on your knees. Keep your (1) _____ straight and your (2) _____ flat on the floor. Breathe in and out slowly and deeply, five to ten times. Next time you breathe in, (3) _____ your arms up over your head. Breathe out, and bring your arms down slowly. Repeat five to seven times.

Dog and Cat This is really two positions, one following the other. For the Dog, begin on your hands and knees. Keep your hands just in front of your (4) _____ with your legs (5) _____ apart as wide as your hips. As you breathe in, angle the (6) _____ up, and curve the spine down, dropping the stomach low, and raise your head up. Now move into the Cat position. Raise the (7) _____ up and angle the hips down, pulling the chest and stomach in again. Repeat several times.

The half shoulder stand Lie on your back and lift your legs up into the air. Place your hands on your (8) _____ for support, resting your elbows and your lower arms on the ground. Make sure your weight is on your (9) _____ and upper back – not your neck. Breathe deeply five to ten times. To come down, slowly lower your legs, keeping them very straight. This will strengthen the (10) _____ in your lower body.

3 **Work in pairs. Ask each other the questions.**

1 Do you use a gym to keep fit?
2 Is there a gym near where you live?
3 How do you feel about taking exercise this way?

17 **4** **Listen to a tour of the sports facilities. Label the plan below with the words in D.**

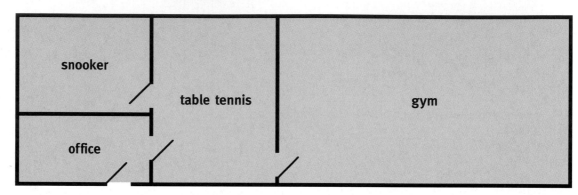

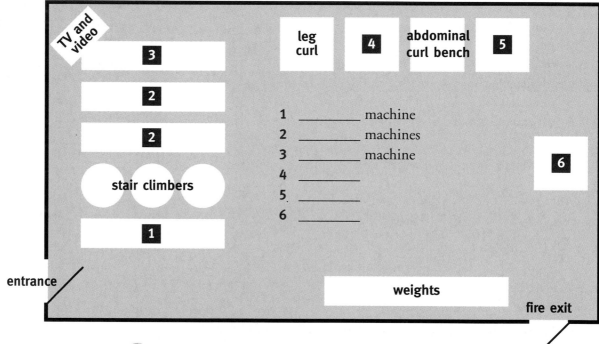

1 _____ machine
2 _____ machines
3 _____ machine
4 _____
5 _____
6 _____

17 **Now listen again and match the machines with the parts of the body.**

1 cardio-vascular machines
2 leg curl bench
3 abdominal curl bench
4 pec deck
5 chin-up bar

a upper arms
b stomach
c chest
d thigh and calf muscles
e heart, lungs and blood flow

Language study: should(n't), must(n't)

5 **Study the example and explanation.**

> *You **should** join as soon as possible ...*
>
> **We use should for less strong suggestions, advice and opinions.**
>
> **Compare these sentences.**
> - *You **must** lose weight or you will have a serious problem.*
> - *You **should** go on a diet; that shirt is too tight for you.*

Now complete the sentences with must, mustn't, should or shouldn't.

1 I think you _____ join the gym.
2 He told them that they _____ return the weights after they use them.
3 You really _____ go home now. I'm going to bed.
4 Before we go jogging we _____ do some stretching exercises.

Pronunciation

18 6 **Listen and notice the pronunciation of should(n't).**

You should join as soon as possible ...

... the first time you use the gym you should do it during the day while I'm here.

... remember you shouldn't put too much weight on the machine ...

You shouldn't try to use this on your own.

18 **Now listen again and practise.**

7 **Complete the sentences.**

1 Good students should _____ .
2 A sportsperson should _____ .
3 Athletes should never _____ .
4 I really must _____ today.
5 In the IELTS test, you mustn't _____ .
6 To learn kendo, you should wear _____ .
7 Good teachers should not _____ .
8 In the library, you shouldn't _____ .
9 To improve your reading skills, you should _____ .
10 To win a blue, you must _____ .

Now work in pairs. Compare your answers.

Reading

IELTS tasks: yes/no/not given; summarising

1   **Label the pictures with the words in E.**

E

t'ai chi
weights
cycling
jogging
juggling

2   **Work in pairs. Decide which statements are true and which are false.**

1   People should concentrate on one area of fitness only.
2   Physical activity is part of our lifestyle.
3   Doing a lot of activity once a month is better than doing a little activity once a day.
4   Walking 10,000 steps a day is good for us.

Now read the passage and check your answers.

3   **Choose the best title for the passage.**

i   Crash-dieting   iii   Better posture
ii   The holistic approach to fitness   iv   Lifestyle choices

Most people know the importance of having a balanced diet. But when it comes to physical exercise, many of us are guilty of crash-routines. In fact, using exercise as a balanced programme of personal fitness is often the last thing people consider as they sign up for gym membership. But exercising purely to burn fat, or to build up muscle size, will not necessarily have a positive effect. Just as a crash-diet can harm your health, so
5   an exercise programme of pure running, or weights, will miss out vital elements. In fact, experts recommend covering five key areas of physical fitness. These are: cardio-vascular exercise such as running, muscular strength, muscular endurance, flexibility, and motor co-ordination from activities like tennis or juggling.

     Victoria Kent, a personal trainer, explains the typical imbalances she encounters among people anxious to start on an exercise programme. 'The classic example is probably the man who just lifts heavy weights,
10   and puts a strain on his heart and cardio-vascular system. But you also get people who just stick to one activity and ignore other areas of exercise. So you might get someone who spends all their time running without doing anything else, and gets overused muscles. They could be more prone to injury because they haven't built up the muscles to protect their limbs from strain and damage. Flexibility is also very important in preventing injury, because tight muscles and joints are more likely to be damaged.'
15   With time a crucial factor for many people, committing to any form of exercise is difficult. But achieving a good level of fitness can be easier than people think. Experts agree that taking a holistic attitude to exercise is a key element of fitness. This means seeing physical exercise as a long-term lifestyle choice, as opposed to a quick fix. Roger Golten is a developer of a form of therapy which aims to increase physical movement. He believes strongly in using the full capacity of your physical abilities on a day-to-day basis.

20 Golten explains the problems he commonly sees in attitudes to exercise: 'People seem to look at losing weight as the universal cure, but adding a few hours in the gym on top of an unhealthy lifestyle is not the way to cure a health problem. Overdoing it is also common. Little and often is better than one big session. Be realistic, progressive and take small steps to begin with. Do something that you enjoy, and think about alternatives such as yoga, t'ai chi, swimming and walking.'

25   For Golten, elements such as posture play a key role in overall health. 'Just sitting better will help you breathe more fully, digest your food better, improve your mobility, self-confidence, energy, voice and presentation, and reduce fatigue, pain and strain on your back, neck, shoulders and arms.' The easiest way to adopt a balanced routine is to become more active in your day-to-day tasks – for example, getting off the bus a stop early, or taking the stairs instead of the lift. Experts recommend walking 10,000 steps a day,

30 although it is estimated that the average adult only does about 3,000.

4 **Read the passage again. Do the statements reflect the claims of the writer?**

Write: YES if the statement reflects the claims of the writer.
       NO if the statement contradicts the claims of the writer.
       NOT GIVEN if it is impossible to say what the writer thinks about this.

1 Table tennis is a good way of improving motor co-ordination.   _____

2 People who only do one kind of activity may be injured more easily. _____

3 Achieving a good level of fitness takes a lot of time and effort.   _____

4 The easiest way to get fit is to be more active in our daily lives.   _____

Now complete the summary. Choose one or two words from the reading passage for each space.

Just doing exercise to lose weight does not guarantee (1) _____ . People need to do a balance of all five fitness activity types. A main element of fitness is a (2) _____ to exercise. Doing a little exercise (3) _____ is better than spending a long time in the gym. The easiest way to get a (4) _____ is to become increasingly active in our daily (5) _____ .

Language study: possibility and certainty

5 **Study the examples and explanations.**

> *So you **might** get someone who spends all their time running …*
> *They **could** be more prone to injury …*   *… a crash-diet **can** harm your health …*
> **We express possibility with verbs like can, could, may and might.**
> *… sitting better **will** help you breathe more fully …*
> *The easiest way to adopt a balanced routine **is** to become more active …*
> **We use is and will to show that we are certain about something.**
> *… tight muscles and joints **are** more **likely to be** damaged.*
> *The classic example **is probably** the man who just lifts heavy weights.*
> **We can also use is/are likely to be, probably and possibly to show possibility.**

Now complete the sentences.

1 People who do not do flexibility exercises _____ .

2 People with good posture _____ .

3 People who do not do any exercise at all _____ .

6 **Work in pairs. Discuss an activity or sport you do or want to try.**

Speaking

F

cricket	
surfing	
American football	
football	

IELTS tasks: individual long turn – descriptions (2); discussion

1   Work in pairs. Decide which equipment A–D is used in the sports in F.

19   Now listen to four descriptions. Put the sports in F in the order you hear them.

19   **2**   Listen again and complete the sentences.

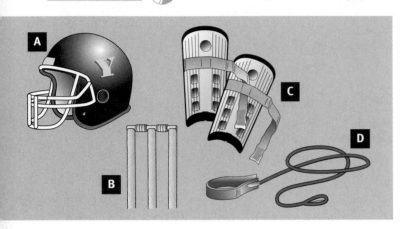

A

B

C

D

1   This piece of equipment _____ to attach your board to your leg … It's usually about ten foot long, _____ nylon.

2   This is _____ leg protection … you _____ them on the lower part of your leg, but only on the front.

3   There are _____ of these, depending on the different player positions. They are made of bars and are _____ the front of the helmet.

4   These are really just three _____ that the bowler tries _____ with a ball.

Now label equipment A–D with the words in G.

G

wicket
leg rope
visor
shin pad

Achieve IELTS: descriptions

If you don't know the name of something, try to describe it. You will get a higher mark if you can do this. You can talk about …

1   the size of the object.   4   what it is used for.

2   the shape of the object.   5   what type or sort of object it is.

3   what it is made of.

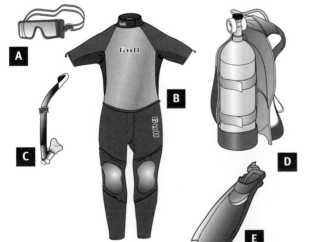

A

B

C

D

E

3   Work in pairs. Student A, turn to assignment 9.1. Describe the object to Student B. Student B, name the object Student A describes.

4   Read the topic below and make notes.

Part 2: Talk about an activity which you enjoy doing in your spare time.

You should say:

1   *what kind of activity it is*

2   *where you usually do it*

3   *what equipment you need to do this*

and say why you enjoy it so much.

Now work in pairs. Student A, you are the examiner; turn to assignment 9.2. Student B, you are the candidate. Follow Student A's instructions.

Writing

IELTS tasks: discursive essay – topic sentences

1   Look at the picture and answer the questions.

1   What do you think it is?
2   How does it work?

Now read the passage and check your answers.

EVERY STEP COUNTS

Forty years ago, the *10,000 steps a day* programme was developed in Japan. Now, several studies in the US have found that walking 10,000 steps a day is an effective way to combat weight gain. It is estimated that the average British person takes 4,000 steps a day. In America, those who take fewer than 5,000 steps daily are classified as unfit. Doing 10,000 steps a day is the equivalent of five miles' walking and burns off in the region of 500 calories. Research shows that this amount of daily walking can help to protect against 20 lifestyle-related illnesses, including heart disease, some cancers and mental illness. Making the time to walk is also a great stress reliever. A cheap way of measuring how we walk are *pedometers*.

Pedometers are activated when your feet hit the floor. A counter then multiplies the total number of steps by the length of a stride to work out the distance covered and therefore the amount of calories burned.

2   Work in pairs. Ask each other these questions.

1   How many steps do you think you walk a day?
2   Would you like a pedometer?
3   Do you have a healthy lifestyle?

3   Read the essay title below and underline the key words.

> *Prevention is better than cure. It is better to spend money on preventing illnesses by promoting healthy living rather than spending it trying to make people better after they are ill.*
>
> To what extent do you agree or disagree with this statement?

4   Work in pairs. Write your main points.

Now write an example for each point.

5 **Read paragraphs A–D in the reading passage. Compare them with your main points.**

A First of all, I'm going to look at people's lifestyles and how this can affect our health. A person's lifestyle can be a major factor in their well-being, both physical and mental. People who eat too much fast, fatty or sugary foods without doing enough physical activity, may put on weight. This has serious effects and can lead to heart disease. Similarly, people who smoke and drink too much run the risk of getting cancers and heart disease. However, by avoiding these things and doing simple things like walking short distances instead of driving, eating five portions of fresh fruit and vegetables a day and taking 20 minutes' exercise three times a week reduces this risk and can prevent disease.

B In conclusion, I would like to argue that people who are healthy should try to stay healthy by avoiding things that cause illnesses, like smoking, and try to keep fit by doing simple activities and eating the correct foods. However, although prevention works for these people, in other cases it may already be too late and the money saved through prevention could be spent researching treatments and cures for these people.

C In this essay I'm going to discuss whether prevention is better than trying to treat people who are ill and whether or not this is possible in all cases. I'm going to divide the subject into illness caused by lifestyle, and illnesses caused by other factors such as genetic factors.

D However, if we now look at genetic factors, the situation is not so clear. Certain genetic factors mean that some people are forced into a lifestyle – for example, people who have certain allergies have to avoid foods containing the thing they react badly to. Obviously, in this case avoiding certain foods as prevention is necessary. Other more serious genetic diseases cannot be treated by prevention and need to be treated medically.

6 **Read the paragraphs again and put them in the right order.**

Paragraph A _____   Paragraph B _____
Paragraph C _____   Paragraph D _____

Now answer the questions.

1 How many main points are there in each paragraph?
2 Where does the main point come in the paragraph?
3 How are the main points introduced?

7 **Read the essay title below and underline the key words.**

> Present a written argument or case for an educated reader with no specialist knowledge of the following topic.
>
> *Modern life is becoming more and more stressful, and many people now suffer from stress-related illnesses. What are the causes of this stress, and what can be done to overcome the problem?*

Now work in pairs. Write your main points and decide on their order.

8 **Write about the topic. You should write at least 250 words.**

RAG week

1 Work in pairs. Look at the pictures and the leaflet. Discuss the connection between them.

RAG week: giving back something to society		
	SATURDAY	great RAG parade and collection, start 1 p.m. city centre
	SUNDAY	raid, market square 12 p.m., sponsored abseil
	MONDAY	speed dating, 7 p.m. Student's Union
	TUESDAY	start of hitch to Dublin, jazz night
	WEDNESDAY	raid – seaside collection
	THURSDAY	24-hour theatre, sponsored parachute jump
	FRIDAY	weekend trip to Amsterdam

Now look at the pictures and decide which events they show.

2 Read the text and circle the correct letter A–C.

Who wrote the text?

A A lecturer.   B A student.   C A member of RAG student committee.

RAG is a fantastic organisation, at many universities across the country. RAG, which stands for *raising and giving*, organises a massive range of fundraising events throughout the year, all of which give students the chance to do something new, make new friends, gain new skills and, most importantly, enjoy themselves. Everything we do raises money for charity through sponsorship, collections and ticket sales.

We regularly run collections in various places around the city (known as *raids*), music events on campus, sponsored parachute jumps and hitchhikes to Dublin and Paris, trips to Amsterdam, and much, much more. All of these are organised and run by volunteers from the university staff and students.

No overview of RAG is complete without a mention of RAG week, the one week of the year when RAG goes mad, and tries to do more than it has ever done before. For the past two years we have raised over £5,000 in the one week of RAG week! The final point to make is, who gets the money? We support a wide range of charities; this group of charities is chosen by our committee of students on a yearly basis, and we donate money to them throughout the academic year.

Now answer the questions.

1 What does *RAG* mean?
2 How many events does RAG organise?
3 How often do students choose the charities to give money to?

A

sponsor
collection
fundraising
support
  (a cause)
donate
volunteer

3 **Read the passage again and match the words in A with the definitions.**

1 to give someone money who is doing something for charity
2 to give money or goods to an organisation like a charity
3 to collect money for a particular purpose
4 an event which is held to make money for charity
5 to help an organisation or person be successful
6 to do work for a charity or organisation for no money

20 4 **Listen to a conversation and circle four letters A–F.**

What do Catherine and James discuss?

A A parade in the city centre.   D Abseiling down a tall building.
B A collection by the Film society.   E A sponsored parachute jump.
C Collecting at a seaside town.   F Hitchhiking to Dublin.

20 5 **Listen again and answer the questions.**

1 Why didn't James volunteer for a raid?
2 Why doesn't he want to collect money at the coast?
3 What is a sponsored hitch?

Express yourself: asking for details

21

Listen and practise the sentences.

What's the catch?   *When's the next raid?*
What does abseiling involve?   *How does that work?*
What do you mean by that?

Now work in pairs. Student A, look at assignment 10.1. Student B, ask for details about the fundraising event.

RAG week
sponsored parachute jump

Date and time:
13 and 14 June at 2 p.m.

Place:
Airfield

Jump from a plane with an
instructor from 3,000 metres.

Reading

IELTS tasks: yes/no/not given; summarising

1   Match the charities with their main purpose.

A   B   C   D   E

1   [This organisation] works with others to overcome poverty and suffering.
2   We believe that the arts have the power to transform lives and communities, and to create opportunities for people …
3   … the promotion of the permanent preservation of lands of historic interest or natural beauty.
4   … to conquer cancer through world-class research.
5   … to develop lasting beneficial relationships with other countries.

Now work in pairs. Discuss the questions.

1   Does your country have any charities similar to these?
2   Do you know anything else about the charities?
3   Are charities an important part of your society?
4   Do you think charities are important in Britain?

2   Read the passage and match the figures with the statements.

1   the income of the Arts Council   a   £7 billion
2   the annual income of charities   b   45 per cent of the total
3   less than 1 per cent of charities   c   £30 billion
4   donations from individuals   d   £500 million
5   a decrease in funding   e   ten years

CHARITABLE TRUSTS

Charities have become a multi-billion-pound concern in Britain. When the first charity law was introduced in 1601 charities simply helped the poor people in the local area. Now there are
5   187,000 registered charities in England and Wales, with an annual income of more than £30 billion. As the average person gives £12.90 a month to charity, the voluntary sector is now as competitive as big business, and as desperate to create brand
10   loyalty as any supermarket giant. The charitable sector is in fact very similar to the retail food industry in the huge differences between the smallest and biggest charities. At the smaller end, nearly a quarter of charities have an income of
15   less than £1,000 a year, or less than 1 per cent of the total income. But at the other extreme, 460 organisations, which represent just 0.28 per cent of the entire sector, have an annual income of

more than £10 million, or 45 per cent of the total income.

The difference between the richest and poorest charities is not necessarily wrong, according to the Charities Aid Foundation. They say that the charitable sector is made up of a huge number of small, community-based groups that really don't need large amounts of money. They believe that the smaller charities are set up for a specific purpose, like building a village hall. They then fold up when they have completed the job. The charities which have millions of pounds have a huge responsibility for providing services in the public sector, which is why they have such a big slice of the funding.

The Arts Council of England is the country's wealthiest charity in terms of income, generating almost £500 million a year. The Arts Council, the British Council, Cancer Research UK, Oxfam and the National Trust are among the top income-generating charities. As well as attracting millions of pounds in public donations, they also receive large government grants for the work they do. For the first time last year, charities received more money from government grants than from public donations. This is not because individual giving is decreasing – it has increased in the past couple of years to more than £7 billion – but because government funding has grown since the government gave more public services to charities to operate.

The voluntary sector is unsure about whether the shift in income from individual donations to government funding is a good or bad development. A spokesperson who represents the National Council for Voluntary Organisations, said: 'In a way it is good because it shows that the government clearly trusts the charitable sector to deliver high-quality public services. The concern is that the political funding could compromise the independence of charities to speak out and protest when they don't agree with government policy.'

The charity world is now rallying after a decade that saw their funding drop due to the popularity of the National Lottery, which gives a lot of money to charities, and damaging stories about their management. Some charities were accused of spending too much money on administration costs and staff. Today more than a quarter of people say they do not give to charity because they do not believe their money will go directly to the cause they want to support.

3   **Read the passage again. Do the statements reflect the claims of the writer?**

Write: YES if the statement reflects the claims of the writer.
    NO if the statement contradicts the claims of the writer.
    NOT GIVEN if it is impossible to say what the writer thinks about this.

1   The world of charities is very similar to the world of supermarkets.   _____

2   The gap between rich and poor charities should be reduced.   _____

3   Charities with millions of pounds have fewer social responsibilities.   _____

4   Charities are receiving more money from businesses.   _____

5   Charities think that more money from the government is both good and bad.   _____

Now complete the summary. Choose one or two words from the reading passage for each space.

The charity world is a multi-billion-pound sector with organisations competing with each other to create (1) _____ . There are (2) _____ between the largest and smallest charities, but this is not (3) _____ . Smaller charities are often founded for a (4) _____ . Large charities receive the biggest amount of money from (5) _____ as they provide services to society. However, money from the political system could affect (6) _____ of charities when they do not agree with government policy.

Language study: giving more information

4   Study the examples and explanations.

> *A spokesperson **who** represents the National Council for Voluntary Organisations ...*
>
> *... small, community-based groups **that** really don't need large amounts of money*
>
> *... have a huge responsibility for providing services in the public sector, **which** is why they have such a big slice of the funding*
>
> **When we want to give more information about a subject or add a reason for something, we can use a relative pronoun. We use *who* for people, *which* or *that* for things, *where* for places and *when* for time.**
>
> *The charities **which** have millions of pounds have a huge responsibility for providing services in the public sector ...*
>
> **When we want to help the other person identify the subject(s) exactly, we use a defining relative clause. We do not put commas around defining relative clauses.**
>
> *... 460 organisations, **which** represent just 0.28 per cent of the entire sector, have an annual income of more than £10 million ...*
>
> **When we want to give additional information about a subject we use a non-defining relative clause. We put commas around non-defining relative clauses.**

Now complete the sentences. Use *who*, *when*, *which* or *that* with correct punctuation.

1   A volunteer / someone / does work without pay.
2   RAG / a student organisation / raises money for charity.
3   Robin / lives in the room next to Tao / a volunteer for Oxfam.
4   Community-based charities / charities / are set up for a specific purpose.
5   The RAG committee has eight members / has its meetings in the Union bar.

5   Work in pairs. Discuss the questions.

1   What is the main source of funding for charities? Why?
2   What are the advantages and disadvantages of this?
3   Why did people stop giving money to charities?

1 Charity begins at home.

2 A bone to the dog is not charity. Charity is the bone shared with the dog, when you are just as hungry as the dog.

(Jack London)

Speaking

IELTS tasks: individual long turn – definitions and examples; discussion

1 Work in pairs. Read the sayings, discuss what they mean and if you agree.

2 Read the topic and rounding-off questions and underline the key words.

> **Part 2: Describe a charity or a good cause.**
>
> *You should say:*
> *1 what the charity or good cause does   2 how it helps people*
> *and why you find this charity or good cause particularly interesting.*

Rounding-off questions.
1 Have you ever given to a charity or good cause?
2 Would you like to work for a charity or good cause?

22/24 3 Listen to three speakers and match the speaker with pictures A–C.

Now work in pairs. Decide which speaker gives the best explanation and why.

23 4 Listen again to Speaker 2. Does he …

1 introduce the topic?	3 give an explanation?	5 give an example?
2 give a definition?	4 ask the examiner questions?	6 give an opinion?

> ## *Achieve IELTS*: giving definitions and examples
>
> Giving definitions and examples can make your contribution clearer and more interesting. We often introduce definitions with a defining relative pronoun. Try to use examples from your country or your personal experience and compare this with what you know about other countries.

Pronunciation

5 **Decide which words are linked.**

*The organisation I'd like to talk about   Let me explain
so it gives them some respect   Who I buy a copy from …*

25 Now listen and practise.

6 Make notes about Part 2 (in task 2) and Part 3.

> **Part 3: Charities and volunteering**
>
> *How important are charities in your country?*
> *Do you think charities should do activities that are really the role of government?*
> *What benefits do you think people get from working with a charity?*

Now work in pairs. Ask each other about topics 1 and 2.

Listening

IELTS tasks: note completion; table completion; multiple-choice questions

CONTACT
volunteer projects

We need students for these projects ...
- health – working on a telephone helpline.
- education – helping children learn to read.
- media – producing a community magazine.
- IT – teaching people to use a computer.
- business – working in a charity shop.
- law – working with the police force.
- languages – working with people new to the community.

1 Work in pairs. Discuss the advantages of doing volunteer work.

2 Read the form and decide which projects you would like to do.

26 **3** Listen to a talk and check your answers to activity 1.

26 **4** Listen to part 1 again and complete the notes. Write no more than three words for each answer.

> Contact develops links with (1) _____ .
>
> Projects
>   Education: volunteer in a (2) _____ .
>   IT: set up (3) _____ and accounting programmes.
>   Retail: assistants in sales, (4) _____ e.g., help with the latest campaign.
>   Languages: many projects need (5) _____ skills.

26 **5** Listen to part 2 again and choose three letters A–E.

1 What does the induction session include?
   A Tea and biscuits.
   B Matching your skills with the projects.
   C Deciding what makes a good volunteer.
   D In-house training from a charity.
   E Meeting the other volunteers.

2 Why is it good to do volunteer work?
   A It develops practical skills learnt in your subject.
   B You can work for a charity.
   C It is good for getting employment.
   D International students can practise their language skills.
   E It makes your life more interesting.

Now work in pairs and ask each other the questions.
   1 Can you think of any more advantages of doing voluntary work?
   2 Have you ever done voluntary work?
   3 Would you like to do voluntary work?

6 Work in pairs. Decide which statements are true (T) and which are false (F).

1 Welfare is better in America than in Europe.	T/F
2 People give more to charity in America than in Europe.	T/F
3 America's political structures are newer than Europe's.	T/F

7 Match the words in B with the definitions.

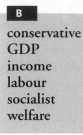

B

conservative
GDP
income
labour
socialist
welfare

1 a belief that people in society should have the same opportunities and the government should own important industries
2 money people get for working
3 a belief in the traditional values of a society
4 the amount of money a country earns (gross domestic product)
5 care provided by an organisation or government for people who need help
6 the workers of a country

27 8 Listen to a lecture and complete the table.

	United States	Europe
the poor are trapped in poverty	29%	(1) _____
luck determines income level	(2) _____	54%
poor people are lazy	60%	(3) _____
welfare spending	(4) _____	45%
giving to charity per person	US$ 700	(5) US$ _____ (not Britain)
political structures	(6) _____	last century

27 9 Listen again circle the correct letters A–C.

1 The last lecture was about …
   A organisations like hospitals and schools.
   B how charities work with governments.
   C attitudes to welfare in Europe and America.

2 In Europe, socialist political parties …
   A are represented better than in America.
   B were set up 200 years ago.
   C have seen many changes.

3 Countries which had war on their territory …
   A limited the power of the labour movement.
   B increased the power of the labour movement.
   C set up new institutions.

10 Work in groups. Discuss the statements.

1 *The poor are trapped in poverty.*
2 *Hard work, not good luck, determines income level.*

Writing

IELTS tasks: discursive essay – introductions and conclusions

1   Work in pairs. Discuss the questions.

1   When do you write the introduction to an essay?
2   What should you include in the introduction?

Now read the title below and underline the key words.

> *Today's charities are taking over duties which are the responsibility of the government. Governments, not charities, are responsible for people's welfare. To what extent do you agree or disagree with this statement?*

2   Read the introduction to an essay and decide if the sentences are true (T) or false (F).

1   The writer will concentrate on the disadvantages of charities.   T/F
2   The government gives charities the right to operate.   T/F
3   Charities need people and organisations to give them money.   T/F

> Nowadays charities are taking a bigger part in providing services to society. This has serious effects in society. In this essay I will look at the advantages and disadvantages of this. First, I would like to say what a charity is and what it does. A charity is an independent organisation (1) _____ is registered with the government, but operates on its own. Charities depend on contributions from donors, people (2) _____ give money to the charity, and other people or organisations (3) _____ contribute money through collections and sponsorship. Charities do work in places (4) _____ there are no social services from the government to help people in need.

Now complete the introduction with *where, which* or *who*.

3   Read the introduction again and order A–D.

A   an outline of the essay
B   a definition
C   why the subject/problem is important
D   background to the title

4   Work in pairs. Discuss the title below.

> *Although giving help to people who need it is thought to be a good thing, in fact many people have stopped giving donations to charities. Today, people do not trust charities. To what extent do you agree or disagree with this statement?*

Now decide what to include from your discussion in the essay.

5   **Write an introduction to the essay in activity 4. Use the framework.**

Nowadays Today These days Recently				
This has some	pros and cons advantages and disadvantages points for and against			
In this essay I	will am going to would like to	write about look at examine outline	the reasons for/behind this. what caused the causes of	First, ... To begin with ...

6   **Read the paragraph. Decide if it is a summary, a conclusion (or both) to the essay title in activity 1.**

> Finally, I'd like to summarise my main points. Today governments have so much to do, if they try to do everything, they just do it badly. This means they need to give responsibilities to other organisations – either private businesses or non-profit making organisations. In my opinion, it is better for non-profit organisations like charities to do this. However, I also believe that these organisations need to stay independent to be able to give valuable advice to governments. In conclusion, I think that charities can take on some government responsibilities but only if their independence is kept.

Now find ...

1   three phrases for giving an opinion.

2   a phrase for summing up.

3   a phrase for concluding.

7   **Write a conclusion for the essay title in task 4. Use the framework below.**

Finally Lastly			
In conclusion (I'd like) to conclude ...	my the	main points	in the essay above
To sum up, (I'd like) to sum up I think that In my opinion I believe (that) It is my belief (that)			

Person wanted

A

waiting staff	kitchen hand
shop assistant	care worker
barista	

1   **Name the job in the picture above. Choose from the words in A.**

   Now match the job in the picture with the advertisement.

2   **Work in pairs. Discuss the questions.**
   1 Which jobs do you think students do?
   2 Do students do part-time jobs in your country?

28 3   **Listen to the conversation and answer the questions.**
   1 Why does Paul need a job?
   2 Why doesn't he want to work in the morning?
   3 Why does he want to do the second job?
   4 Which job does he apply for?

   Now listen again and complete the job advertisements.

28 4   **Read the advertisements again and find words that mean ...**
   1 full of energy.
   2 someone you can trust to work well.
   3 someone who thinks about the feelings of other people.
   4 a person who is interested in doing something and wants to do it.
   5 a strong feeling of excitement.

Language study: preference

5   **Study the examples and explanation.**

> *I'd rather not work in the morning ...*   *I wouldn't want to work at night ...*
> *I wouldn't mind working at the weekend ...*   *I('d) prefer to work in the afternoon.*
>
> **We use *would* (*not*) + *rather/prefer/mind/want* to talk about possible options.**

POSITIONS VACANT

JOB AVAILABLE IN FAMILY RESTAURANT.
Must be reliable with some (1) _____
Competitive wage.
Tel 041 222 852

---

(2) _____
ASSISTANT REQUIRED FOR BAKERY.
(3) _____ player, days and nights.
Call 041 700 258

POSITION VACANT FOR CARING PERSON.
Casual weekend shift (4) (_____ a.m.).
Must be considerate and friendly.
Phone (5) _____

PERSON NEEDED FOR BUSY COFFEE BAR.
Enthusiastic, lively!
Afternoons and evenings only.
Phone Stuart on 040 906 190

WAITER REQUIRED FOR BUSY CAFÉ.
Salary negotiable.
Must be energetic and well-motivated.
Ring 040 931 602

Now complete the sentences.

1 When I finish studying I _____ an office job to a manual job.
2 I _____ work from home than work in an office.
3 Aiko _____ working late, as long as it doesn't happen too often.
4 I _____ to work in the spring vacation as I need to prepare for the exams.

Pronunciation

29 **6** **Listen and mark the way the voice rises and falls in the sentences in 5.**

29 **Now listen again and practise.**

7 **Work in pairs. Discuss which job in 1 you would prefer and why.**

Now discuss the questions.

1 Have you ever had a part-time job?
2 Have you ever been to a job interview?
3 What kinds of questions do you think people ask in interviews?

30 **8** **Listen to an interview and complete the application form.**

30 **9** **Listen again and circle the correct answer A–C.**

1 The Canberra Care Agency started as …
   A government organisation.
   B a private agency.
   C a voluntary organisation.

3 The agency …
   A only works with people in Canberra.
   B only works with people in university accommodation.
   C tries to put people together who live close to each other.

2 How does Paul think his interests will help in the job?
   A Because it will help him to socialise.
   B Because he is good at gardening.
   C Because he is a member of the student radio station.

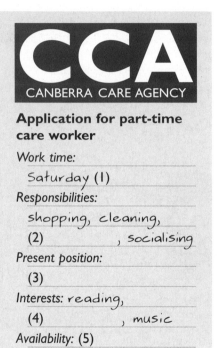

CCA
CANBERRA CARE AGENCY

Application for part-time care worker

Work time:
  Saturday (1)
Responsibilities:
  shopping, cleaning,
  (2) _____, socialising
Present position:
  (3)
Interests: reading,
  (4) _____, music
Availability: (5)

31

Express yourself: saying goodbye

Listen and complete the sentences.

1 Well thank you very much _____ . It was very _____ to meet you.
2 Yes, thanks for coming. Have a good _____ back.
3 Good to meet you _____ . _____ to see you again soon.

Now practise the sentences.

---

10 **Work in groups of three. Choose a job from task 1 and hold an interview for it.**

- Students A and B: you are the interviewers. Prepare questions to ask Student C.
- Student C: you are applying for the job. Prepare two questions to ask the interviewers.

Reading

IELTS tasks: multiple-choice questions; true/false/not given

1   **Work in pairs. Ask each other the questions.**

Do you know …

1 anyone who works at home instead of in an office?   2 anyone who works long hours?

3 anyone who is stressed because of work or study?

2   **Look at the picture and the title of the passage. Write three things you think the passage contains.**

Now read the passage and check your answers.

THE BALANCED WORKERS OF TOMORROW

Work-life balance is the buzzword of the moment. Last week was the fourth annual Work-Life Balance week in which a record two million employees took part. Meanwhile, forward-looking organisations are boasting of their work-life programmes. But can raising awareness of work-life balance – recognising employees as real people with personal lives, responsibilities and interests – have a real impact on the workplace? Getting the balance right depends on convincing employers of the benefits and making sure workers are confident enough to ask for changes to their conditions in the current job market. After all, a worker who did not feel secure in his or her workplace would not ask for better working conditions.

Recent working proposals have increased parental leave and given certain workers the right to have their requests for flexible working at least considered. However, these guidelines fall far short of being made law. What seems like common sense – that if there were more satisfied employees this would result in less absenteeism, stress-related illness and staff turnover – is backed up by a growing number of studies. It has been calculated that 30 per cent of sick leave in Britain is attributed to stress, anxiety and depression – all made worse by poor work–life balance. The annual cost to the UK health service of stress-related illness is £2 billion, while this year it has been estimated that the cost of stress-related absence reached $300 billion a year in the US and $200 million in Australia.

Given the current assessment, it may well be a generation before more holistic attitudes to employees are accepted. Indeed, the focus is now shifting to the next generation of workers by highlighting the pressures on younger people thinking about entering the workforce or already juggling part-time work with their studies. A poor economy has done little to encourage job-seekers to bargain for better conditions. Job insecurity and unemployment have changed attitudes, particularly at the younger end of the job market. So would the next generation fight for better conditions if it came to changing their working lives? For some school leavers their anxiety over finding work was far greater than the strain that they feared work may bring to their lives. They believed that if they did not do the job, then someone else would do it instead of them.

Can anything be done to improve this critical situation? Flexible work arrangements, part-time work, job-sharing, home-based work and paid parental leave are all examples of family-friendly practices that help people to balance their lives. In order to have a more balanced life, more and more people are choosing to work from home at least some of the time, but there are many new dangers – overworking, lack of communication with the office and negative impact on home life are examples of the problems with home-based work. The biggest obstacle to balancing work and home life seems to be attitude: organisations and the people they employ need to recognise that work–life balance can actually improve productivity without significant investment. Many workers would be happy to work their hours, if they could get back some control over their busy lives. In the meantime, experts vary in their advice for strategies for balancing our work and lives.

3   Match the words in B with the definitions.

1   feeling worried about something
2   the number of people who enter and leave an organisation
3   the way people think or feel about something
4   not at a place of work or study
5   permission to be away from work

4   Read the passage again and choose four letters A–F.

A good work–life balance means …

A   seeing employees as real people.
B   giving workers rights.
C   reducing costs to industry.
D   highlighting pressures on young people.
E   more and more people working from home.
F   improving production.

Now find words and phrases in the passage that mean …

1   the effect something has.
2   to support an idea.
3   to look at a situation and make a judgement.
4   to be able to make changes and deal with a changing situation.
5   a situation that is becoming dangerous.

5   Read the passage again. Do the statements agree with the information given in the reading passage?

**Write: TRUE if the statement is true according to the passage.
       FALSE if the statement is false according to the passage.
       NOT GIVEN if the statement is not given in the passage.**

1   Employers need to think flexible working is a good
    idea for workers to ask them to change the way
    they work.   _____

2   Studies show that office workers are better paid.   _____

3   Some young people are trying to balance studies and
    part-time work.   _____

4   People who work at home do not get enough exercise.   _____

5   There are no negative effects to working at home.   _____

6   Work in pairs. Ask each other the questions.

1   What are the advantages and disadvantages of working at home?
2   Would you prefer to work at home or in an office?

Language study: second conditional

7   Study the examples and explanation.

> ... *if there* **were** *more satisfied employees this would result in less absenteeism* ...
>
> ... *if they* **did not do** *the job, then someone else would do it instead* ...
>
> **We use second conditionals to talk about situations that we can imagine in the future.**
>
> *if* + past (*not*) + *would* (*not*) + present
>
> **Questions**
>
> ... **would** *the next generation fight for better conditions* **if** *it came to changing their working lives?*
>
> *would* (*not*) + present + *if* + past (*not*)?

Now complete the sentences using the words in brackets.

1   If Liz _____ a choice, she _____ at home more often. (have/work)

2   _____ you _____ your job if there _____ too much stress? (leave/be)

3   If I _____ a job, I _____ for one. (not have/apply)

4   My ideal job _____ one which _____ a good salary and not many hours. (be/have)

5   I _____ that job if you _____ me a million pounds. (not do/pay)

bee keeper

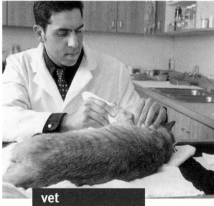
vet

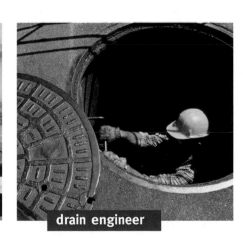
drain engineer

8   Work in pairs. Ask each other the questions.

1   Which job would you do?

2   Which job would you never do?

3   Which job would you do if ...

   A   they gave you a lot of money?

   B   you had special clothing?

   C   you didn't have to work very hard/do it very often?

Listening

IELTS tasks: table completion; note completion

C

CV
job-hunting
occupation
recruitment
training
vocation

1 Match the words in C with the definitions.

1 looking for a job
2 a short description of your education, work experience and interests
3 a person's job or profession
4 a job which often involves helping other people
5 finding and selecting people for work
6 learning the skills necessary to do something

2 Work in pairs. Decide which things the Careers Advice Service does.

1 Arranges visits to employers.
2 Takes students to recruitment fairs.
3 Trains students how to write a CV.
4 Writes letters to employers for students.
5 Interviews students and gives them advice.
6 Gives jobs to students.

32 3 Listen to a conversation in the Careers Advice Service and label the plan.

32 Now listen again and complete the table with no more than three words for each answer.

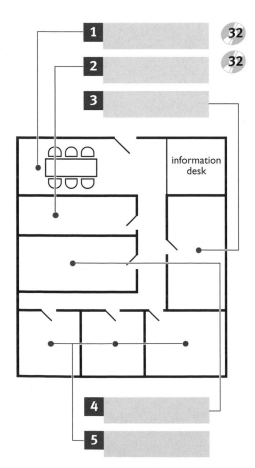

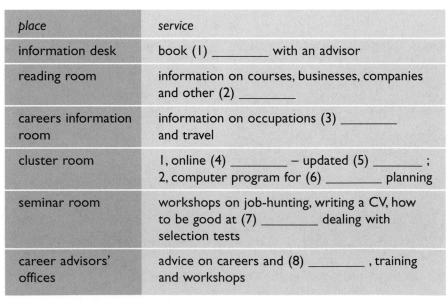

place	service
information desk	book (1) _____ with an advisor
reading room	information on courses, businesses, companies and other (2) _____
careers information room	information on occupations (3) _____ and travel
cluster room	1, online (4) _____ – updated (5) _____ ; 2, computer program for (6) _____ planning
seminar room	workshops on job-hunting, writing a CV, how to be good at (7) _____ dealing with selection tests
career advisors' offices	advice on careers and (8) _____ , training and workshops

4 Work in pairs. Answer the questions.

1 What is the starting point for students who use the Careers Advice Service?
2 How does the careers computer program work?
3 When should students see a careers advisor and why?

Now discuss which part of the Careers Advice Service you think is the most helpful.

5   Work in pairs. Ask each other the questions.

1   Are you good at tests?   2   How do you prepare for tests?

3   Do you like word games and puzzles?

6   Complete the sentences with the words and phrases in D.

1   _____ is connected with using logic.

2   _____ is connected with using charts and diagrams.

3   _____ is connected with ability to work or study.

4   _____ is connected with using words.

5   _____ is connected with using mathematics.

D
verbal reasoning
numerical reasoning
diagrammatical reasoning
abstract reasoning
aptitude

33   7   Listen to the careers advisor's talk and tick the correct column.

	aptitude test	personality test
has a time limit		
has multiple-choice questions		
has no correct answer		
the person's score is compared with other people's scores		
has many parts		
honesty is important		

8   Read the notes below and discuss the possible answers.

33   Now listen again and complete the notes. Write no more than three words for each answer.

Psychometric tests (1) _____ the mind. They were developed at (2) _____ the 20th century and used in business from the 1970s.

There are different kinds of aptitude test.

- Verbal: a passage with a (3) _____ .
- Numerical: about mathematical ability.
- Diagrammatic: test how good you are (4) _____ diagrams.
- Abstract reasoning: tests (5) _____ thinking.

The earlier a test is used the (6) _____ it is.

Preparation: practice tests, (7) _____ games, mathematical games.

Personality tests: find out about your character from (8) _____ to questions and statements.

Focus on teamwork, honesty, motivation and (9) _____ to life.

Purpose: make sure candidate will enjoy the company culture and (10) _____ .

9   Work in pairs. Discuss the questions.

1   Why do some employers ask people to take these tests?

2   Do you think these tests are necessary?

3   Do employers in your country test people before they employ them?

Writing

IELTS tasks: discursive essay – examples and definitions

1   **Label pictures A–C with the words in E.**

Now work in pairs. Discuss the differences between the kinds of industries.

2   **Read the title below and underline the key words.**

> *Since the 18th century technological advances have replaced people in the workplace. With today's technology this process is happening at a greater rate. Technology is increasingly responsible for unemployment. To what extent do you agree or disagree with this statement?*

3   **Read an answer to the title in 2 and complete the notes.**

A

B

C

Technological advances always have an impact on people at work. Sometimes it can mean that people are no longer necessary in their job, but sometimes they make people's work easier. We can define technology as scientific knowledge used for practical purposes in industry and
5   commerce. I would also like to make a further distinction between this and high technology, which is electronic or information technology.

In my view, technology really began to have an effect on industry in the early part of the twentieth century with the invention of two processes: automation, or the use of machines to do work previously
10   done by people, and assembly-line production. Assembly-line production means that a product is built in different stages by people or machines. The result of this was that certain industries like the car industry did not need as many people, as automated machines and robots were able to do jobs such as painting the car, or putting the car together.
15   However, if we now turn to look at the effect of high technology on the workplace, in my view there has been a different effect. It is true that computers are able to do some things that people used to do, an example is answering and directing telephone calls, but I believe that advances in high technology have made people's working lives better
20   through improvements in communications. First, things like e-mail and the Internet mean that people can work faster and more efficiently. For example, people working in service industries like banking use computers much more than pen and paper nowadays. Second, some work can be done from home, which means that people do not need to spend time
25   travelling and can work where and when they want to.

In conclusion, technology has resulted in unemployment in some traditional industries like the car industry. On the other hand, in other industries such as service industries, technology – especially high technology – has improved the way we work.

Introduction: definitions
- (1) _____ – scientific knowledge used for practical purposes
- (2) _____ – e.g., electronic or information technology

Point 1: technology
    Two processes (3) _____ and (4) _____ eg, (5) _____

Point 2: high technology
- (6) _____ are able to do some things instead of people, eg, (7) _____
- communication improvements (8) _____ , (9) _____

Conclusion:
    technology has caused (10) _____ , but has also brought some improvements

Now read the passage again and underline phrases for giving definitions and examples.

Achieve IELTS: giving examples

You will be given a mark for arguments, ideas and evidence. Give examples for all your ideas. Do not use *etc.*, *and so on* or other expressions like these. It appears lazy to the reader.

4 **Complete the sentences. Use these words and phrases.**

such as   *for example*   *like*

1 In the 1980s some computer software companies _____ Microsoft expanded rapidly.
2 In 2001, accounting procedures in some American businesses were very bad. _____ , Enron.
3 Many businesses are environmentally friendly with practices _____ recycling paper.

5 **Read the essay title and underline the key words.**

> *The traditional idea of working for the same company for life in one particular place is changing. Today people work for different companies, in different jobs and in different ways. Unfortunately, this also leads to job insecurity and uncertainty about the future. Do you agree or disagree?*

6 **Work in pairs. Make notes on the topic in 5.**

Now write 250 words. You have 40 minutes.

Speaking

IELTS tasks: introduction; individual long turn; discussion – giving opinions

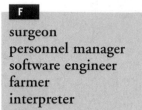

F

surgeon
personnel manager
software engineer
farmer
interpreter

1 Decide which jobs in F involve ...

   1 working with people/computers/animals/languages.
   2 working in agriculture/retail/manufacturing/health/government.

2 Read the words and phrases in G and decide what are the most and least important things in a job.

34 **3** Listen to the conversation and number the words and phrases in G in the order you hear them.

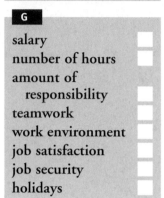

G

salary ☐
number of hours ☐
amount of
   responsibility ☐
teamwork ☐
work environment ☐
job satisfaction ☐
job security ☐
holidays ☐

Language study: opinions

4 Study the examples.

Personally,	*I think (that) ...*	*Actually, I've changed my mind.*
Actually,	*I believe ...*	*I don't know really.*
In fact,		
Do you want to know what I think?		*What do you think?*
In my view/opinion ...		*What's your view/opinion?*
My opinion is (that) ...		*What about?*

Now work in pairs. Discuss the words and phrases in G and make a new list.

5 Read the topic below, underline the key words and make notes on part 2.

> **Part 1: Let's talk about your home town ...**
> *1 Is it a large or small place?*
> *2 What is the most interesting thing about it?*
> *3 What kind of jobs do most people do?*
>
> **Part 2: Describe a job you have done or would like to do.**
> *You should say ...*
> *1 what is involved in the job*
> *2 what qualities and qualifications you need to get the job*
> *and explain why you would like to do it.*
> *Is it easy to get this kind of job? What are the best things about it?*
>
> **Part 3: Let's consider, first of all, work in your country ...**
> *1 How is the workplace changing in your country?*
> *2 Which jobs do people value most in your county?*
> *3 Which are the most important jobs to your country's economy?*

Now work in pairs. Student A, you are the examiner; interview Student B. Student B, you are the candidate; answer the questions.

Seminar

1 Work in pairs. Ask each other the questions.

1 Have you ever been to a workshop, lecture or seminar?
2 Are you punctual or are you often late?
3 Do you occasionally forget to do homework?
4 Do you occasionally forget appointments?
5 Have you ever made an excuse? What was the worst excuse you ever heard?

2 Listen to a conversation and choose A–C.

1 Does the conversation take place …
   A in a café?   B during a tutorial?   C during a seminar?

2 How many people are going to give a presentation?
   A Two.   B Three.   C Four.

3 Does the tutor …
   A become angry with Paul?
   B ask Paul to give his presentation later?
   C ask Paul to summarise the main points of his presentation?

35 3 Listen again and tick the excuses Paul gives.

1 He didn't set his alarm clock.
2 He feels ill.
3 He left his pen on the bus.
4 He lost his presentation.
5 He forgot about the presentation.

Express yourself: apologies and excuses

36 **Listen and practise the phrases and sentences.**

I'm so sorry I'm late.   I apologise for interrupting you …   I'm very sorry.
It completely slipped my mind.   I absolutely forgot it's for today.
I was convinced it's for next week.   I really can't remember them, I'm afraid.

Now work in pairs. Student A, ask Student B for …

1 today's homework.   2 their project.   3 their presentation.   4 their text book.

Student B, apologise and give an excuse.

4   **Read the e-mail below and answer the questions.**

1 Why was Paul late?
2 How did he feel when the tutor asked for his presentation?
3 What does the tutor think?

Lily,

It's been one of the worst days of my life. My tutorial was absolutely awful. First of all I was late. I told the Prof that I missed my alarm call, but he didn't believe me. Then I had to borrow a pen. After that, Prof Miles asked for outlines of our projects and told me that I was going to give a presentation for that tutorial. I had no idea. My memory is just so bad — I thought it was for next week. But the worst thing was when the Prof asked me for a summary of the main points. I was so embarrassed. I'm sure Prof Miles thinks I haven't done a thing because I couldn't even remember the title of the project, never mind give a rundown of the main points. What am I going to do about this? Help!

Paul

Now read the passage again. Underline the phrases that show how Paul felt.

5   **Decide which three words in A mean *a brief description*.**

A

project
outline
presentation
summary
rundown

37 6   **Listen to a conversation and circle three letters A–E.**

A Carmen had 15 minutes of questions about her presentation.
B Lily suggests making a list of regular things to do.
C Paul should go to the gym.
D He should make a short-term plan.
E He has forgotten about a test.

37   **Now listen again and complete the table. Write no more than three words for each answer.**

Study timetable	
Weekly preparation	lectures, (1) _____ and seminars reading list, list of (2) _____
Long-term work	(3) _____ and exams

7   **Write a study timetable for yourself.**

Now work in pairs. Compare your timetables.

Listening

IELTS tasks: note completion; multiple-choice questions

1   Do the quiz.

LEARNING TYPES

What kind of learner are you? How do you best remember new information? Try this quiz and find out.

1   When you spell, do you …
A   try to see the word?
B   say the word aloud?
C   try to write the word?

2   When you concentrate, are you …
A   disturbed by untidiness?
B   disturbed by sounds or music?
C   disturbed by activity around you?

3   When you meet someone again, do you …
A   forget names but remember faces or remember where you met?
B   forget faces but remember names or remember what you talked about?
C   remember what you did together?

4   When you read, do you …
A   like descriptive scenes and like to imagine what is happening?
B   enjoy conversations and try to hear the characters?
C   prefer action stories or don't like reading?

5   When you do something new, do you …
A   like to see diagrams or pictures?
B   prefer to hear instructions or like to talk about it with someone else?
C   prefer to jump right in and try it?

Now turn to assignment 12.1 and read your results. Work in pairs and discuss your answers.

38   2   **Listen to a lecture and write the appropriate letters A–C against the questions.**

A: long-term memory   B: short-term memory   C: immediate memory

1   Holds information for less than a second.   _____
2   Holds information for less than 30 seconds.   _____
3   Holds seven items.   _____
4   Stores unlimited information.   _____
5   Is divided into two kinds.   _____

Now match the words in B with the definitions.

1   the ability to remember facts
2   repeating something aloud in order to remember it
3   bringing back information to use it again
4   to pay attention to information and remember it

> **B**
>
> retention
> retrieval
> rehearsal
> registration

38 **3** **Listen again and complete the notes. Write no more than three words for each answer.**

Information needs to be (1) _____ so that it can be used later. The three Rs of memory are (2) _____ , retention and retrieval. We compare information in our immediate or (3) _____ . The short-term memory is used to (4) _____ , eg, telephone numbers. The long-term memory is divided into episodic and semantic memories. The episodic is the (5) _____ telling part; the semantic memory remembers (6) _____ , eg, the name of a mountain or city.

Retrieval: you can better remember things you heard about if you have a good (7) _____ . A good (8) _____ memory means you better remember things you see.

4 **Work in pairs. Discuss which things can help you study.**

▪ being interested in the subject   ▪ listening to music
▪ writing things down   ▪ sleeping
▪ drinking water   ▪ reviewing your work
▪ taking short breaks from studying   ▪ relaxing
▪ avoiding food with lots of sugar   ▪ being positive

39 **Now listen to a seminar and tick the things you hear.**

39 **5** **Listen again and choose A–C.**

1 The talk is about …
   A making a study timetable.   B good study techniques.   C relaxation activities.

2 It helps to …
   A drink water and eat foods that contain protein.
   B drink water and eat foods that contain carbohydrates.
   C eat food that contains protein and carbohydrates.

3 When we sleep our brain …
   A has a short break.
   B keeps information and makes sense of it.
   C dreams about what happened that day.

4 Learning is easier if we …
   A feel good.   B think about something else.   C study a difficult subject.

5 Students should revise because …
   A they make mistakes.
   B 70 per cent of the information we learn is gone the next day.
   C they can do better in tests.

6 **Work in pairs. Ask each other the questions.**

1 Which things in task 4 do you do?
2 Which things would you like to do?
3 Do you know any other good study techniques?

Writing

IELTS tasks: discursive essay – proofreading

1 Work in pairs. Ask each other this question.

What do you need to pay special attention to when you finish a piece of writing?
1 Your spelling.   2 Your punctuation.   3 Your grammar.   4 Your vocabulary.

2 Read the title below and underline the key words.

> *In some traditions memorising information given to students by a teacher is an important method of learning. Other educational traditions ask students to find information by themselves and place little importance on remembering it. The role of memory in education is unimportant. Do you agree with this?*

Now read a student's answer and match the paragraphs with the summaries.

summary	*paragraph*
1 The role of memorising in different cultures.	_____
2 Balancing different ways of learning.	_____
3 Memorising during school years.	_____
4 Memorising during early childhood.	_____

A I think that all our life is founded on memorising. We start memorising from the day we are born. We learn everything from our parents by memory. For example, we listen to them talking to us, we remember and learn how to speak. Watching what our parents do teaches us how to behave. Likewise, when we ask children what's on a picture (if it's a leon or a
5 cat) we want them to memorise and remember what we say.
B Later, in scools, however, the question is how to memorise and what to memorise. There is a big difference between the modern western-european way and the old-fashioned eastern-European way. In eastern Europe children are asked to memorise a lot. They have to remember what they learnt from their teachers and from books. In contrast, children in
10 western contryes are more open and free in express themselves but many times their knowledge of language or of the world does not have a strong basis. For example, you can't study history without memorising some key information like dates and names.
C With foreign languages, a few people have the ability to remember a word once listened, but people who don't have this skill and have no opportunity of travel have to memorise
15 new words. I can remember my first language lesson when we memorised a hole dilog and it was really great to feel that I was speaking italian. After this first period, I think it is wrong to memorise texts, but unfortunately this was the way of doing things with eastern countyes. This method doesn't let you to find your way of expressing yourself and you will still be afraid to talk in an open discussion.
20 D I think extrimes are never good. We should develop our imagination and discover the world ourselves but the same time we should use and train our brains to learn (memorise) and have a good basic knowledge of the world around us.

3 **Decide what the student's main point is. Circle A–C.**

A Western and Eastern education is different.

B Memorising is necessary in our early years, but we should discover things ourselves later.

C To learn a language we need a good memory.

Now work in pairs. Decide if you agree or disagree with the writer.

4 **Read the passage again and ...**

1 find eight spelling mistakes.

2 find two places where capital letters need to be used (paragraphs B and C).

3 find three vocabulary mistakes and replace them with *often* (paragraph B), *immediately* (paragraph C), or *mind* (paragraph D).

Now correct the grammar mistakes.

1 wrong preposition (paragraphs A and C)

2 no gerund (paragraphs A, B and C)

3 wrong use of infinitive (paragraph C)

Achieve IELTS: assessing your essay

When you have finished the essay read it again and ask yourself these questions.

1 Have I answered the question or have I gone away from the topic?

2 Is the essay well structured and clear?

3 Can the reader understand my main points?

4 Are there any spelling, punctuation, vocabulary or grammar mistakes?

---

5 **Work in pairs. Read the title below and underline the key words.**

> *Without intelligence it is impossible to be successful academically. Intelligence is the most important factor in academic success. Do you agree or disagree with the statement?*

Now work in pairs. Discuss the title and make notes and an essay plan.

6 **Write the essay. You have 40 minutes.**

Now work in pairs.

Student A, give your essay to Student B and take their essay. Student B, give your essay to Student A and take their essay. Check each other's essay for spelling, punctuation, vocabulary and grammar.

Reading

IELTS tasks: matching headings and paragraphs; true/false/not given; summarising

C

burgundy
black
yellow
purple
grey
turquoise

1 **Match the words in C with the pictures.**

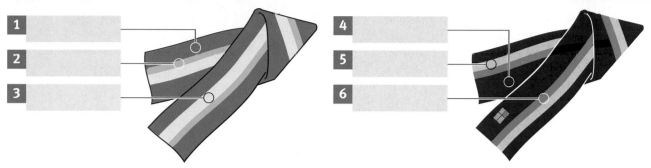

2 **Work in pairs. Answer the questions.**

1 What is your favourite colour and why?

2 What does the colour make you think of?

3 Can you describe it in more detail (how it feels, looks, sounds and/or smells)?

3 **Read the title of the passage. Decide what the passage is about.**

Now read the passage and choose the most suitable headings for sections A–D.

Headings

i   Current research into synaesthesia
ii Future research
iii What is synaesthesia?
iv Experiments into synaesthesia
v   The history of synaesthesia
vi The effects of synaesthesia
vii The study and its findings

Synaesthesia: mixing the senses

A Synaesthesia is a condition that raises more questions than answers. For people with this condition, the word *Tuesday* may be yellow, the middle C note on a piano could smell of earth and the word *grass* might be the colour purple. Now scientists from the University of Melbourne are researching synaesthesia by analysing brain images of people with this condition. It is one of the first objective analyses of synaesthesia and their results have begun to reveal the secrets of how the brain functions. The university has 200 synaesthetes on its database – the largest in the world – and it estimates there could be as many as 1 in 2,000 people with this condition.

B 'Many synaesthetes don't realise they have the condition. They are unaware that the way they perceive the world is different,' says Anina Rich, the scientist who is conducting the research. In most people, a physical stimulus presents a single sensation: light gives us a visual sensation, sound an auditory sensation, smell an olfactory sensation. Synaesthetes, however, get an extra one or more sensations. For example, a particular sound might cause them to experience a colour, taste or smell. This extra layer of information may be behind synaesthetes' excellent memory. 'They have colour as an extra bit of information to help them remember things like names and strings of numbers,' says Rich. The literature is also full of assertions that synaesthetes tend to be creative, artistic and highly emotional individuals.

C The scientists are focusing on the most common form of synaesthesia where digits, letters or words elicit specific colours when they are seen or heard. Rich describes one woman who told her: 'If I think about the word *grass*, I know the object we call grass is green, but to me the word grass is purple because it starts with *G* and the letter G is a purple letter for me.' Rich believes the experiences occur without conscious effort and start happening from early childhood and they are highly consistent over time. Rich said that one lady saw most of her letters as different, but specific, shades of burgundy. These shades stayed the same over the years. Another person said they sometimes got people's names mixed up. For example, they may call someone Debbie when that person is really called Paula because D and P are more or less the same colour green for them.

D Using Magnetic Resonance Imaging, the team recorded brain images from a group of synaesthetes and non-synaesthetes as they performed a series of visual tasks to find out which areas of the brain are involved. The study found that although one area of the brain was particularly active, in people with

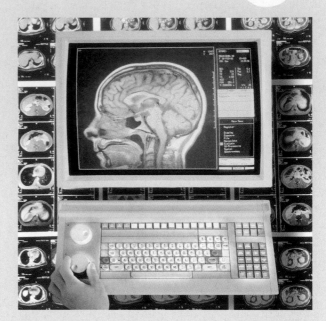

synaesthesia several parts of the brain were active during the experiment. Rich said 'Synaesthesia crosses cultures, affects six times as many women as men, and appears to have a genetic component. Many of our participants are artists or musicians. There is certainly an anecdotal link with creativity. For the vast majority, there is little or no interference from synaesthetic experiences in daily life.'

---

4   **Do the statements agree with the information given in the reading passage?**

   Write: TRUE if the statement is true according to the passage.
   FALSE if the statement is false according to the passage.
   NOT GIVEN if the statement is not given in the passage.

   1   The study is beginning to show how the brain works.   _____

   2   Synaesthetes have calendars to help them remember.   _____

   3   Synaesthetes are forgetful.   _____

   4   The sensations stay the same over long periods of time.   _____

   5   The condition may be passed from parents to children.   _____

5   **Find words in the passage which mean ...**

   1   to show something new (paragraph A).   _____

   2   something that causes a reaction (paragraph B).   _____

   3   physical or emotional feelings (paragraph B).   _____

   4   not changing during a long time (paragraph C).   _____

   5   part of a larger thing (paragraph D).   _____

6 **Complete the table with words from the passage.**

sight	(1) _____
taste	oral
sound	(2) _____
(3) _____	olfactory
touch	kinaesthetic

Now read the passage again and complete the summary. Choose one or two words from the passage for each space.

Scientists began to research synaesthesia by looking at (1) _____ taken from people with the condition. Most people are not aware that their (2) _____ things is not the same as other people. For synaesthetes a physical stimulus causes more than one sensation and this may be the reason for their very good (3) _____ . The condition starts in childhood and stays (4) _____ over many years. Synaesthesia is found across cultures and is more common in (5) _____ than in men.

Language study: gerunds

7 **Study the examples and explanation.**

> *Using Magnetic Resonance Imaging, the team recorded brain images …*
>
> *… the experiences occur without conscious effort and start **happening** from early childhood …*
>
> *… by **analysing** brain images …*
>
> **We use gerunds at the start of a sentence or clause, after certain verbs and after prepositions.**

Now complete the sentences using a gerund or an infinitive.

1 Not many people have admitted _____ different colours for different numbers. (see)
2 Can you imagine _____ synaesthesia? (have)
3 I'm planning _____ some research using Magnetic Resonance Imaging. (do)
4 Sara's just finished _____ her report on memory and forgetting. (plan)

Pronunciation

40 **8** **Listen and practise, paying attention to the / ŋ / sound.**

9 **Work in groups. Discuss the questions.**

1 Which information in the passage did you find interesting?
2 Why do you think artistic people are more likely to experience synaesthesia?
3 How does synaesthesia help people remember?
4 Have you ever had an experience like this?

Speaking

IELTS tasks: introduction; individual long turn; discussion – rephrasing

1   **Answer the questions for yourself.**

	You	Speaker 1	Speaker 2	Speaker 3	Your partner
1 Do you have a good memory?					
2 Have you got a good memory for …					
A names?					
B faces?					
C dates?					
3 What was the last thing you forgot?					

41   **Now listen to three people and complete the table.**

Express yourself: rephrasing

41   **Listen and practise the expressions.**

What I mean to say is …   *Let me put it another way …*
… by that …   *To put it differently …*
In other words …

Now work in pairs. Ask each other the questions in 1 and complete the table for your partner.

2   **Match the sayings with the meanings.**

1 I can't remember off the top of my head.

2 It's on the tip of my tongue.

3 Can you jog my memory?

4 Paul racked his brains thinking about the subject of his essay.

5 You took the words out of my mouth.

a You said exactly what I wanted to say.

c At this moment I can't remember.

b Can you help me to remember?

d I can almost remember it.

e He tried very hard to remember the subject of his essay.

Now work in pairs. Discuss any similar sayings in your language.

3 Read the candidate task card below. Decide what the overall topic is about.

Part 1: Introduction.

1 Where are you studying at the moment?

2 Which subjects are you studying?

3 What do you find are the easiest and the most difficult things about studying?

Part 2: Describe your approach to studying.

You should say:

1 where you study best

2 how long you study for each day/week

3 any study techniques you use.

You have one minute to think about what you are going to say. You can make some notes to help you.

Rounding-off questions.

1 Which study techniques would you recommend to other students?

2 Which study techniques are good for people studying languages?

Part 3: Let's consider how attitudes in education have changed.

1 Is remembering information by heart still important in your education system?

2 Do you think remembering things by heart is a useful skill?

Finally, let's talk about remembering.

Do you think having a good memory is important?

---

4 Work in pairs. Student A, you are the examiner; interview Student B. Student B, you are the candidate; answer the questions.

Now change roles. Student B, you are the examiner; interview Student A. Student A, you are the candidate; answer the questions.

Assignments

UNIT 1 On course

Assignment 1.1

Student A

Here is a complete weekly timetable. Student B has a partially completed timetable, and will ask you questions so that they can complete it.

		Monday	Tuesday	Wednesday	Thursday	Friday
a.m.	time	10–11	9–10	10–11	10–12	9–11
	subject	Organisational Behaviour	Languages for Business – Chinese	Study skills	Principles of Business	Foundations of Production
	room	Main lecture hall	Language laboratory	Seminar room 1	Main lecture hall	Lecture room 2
p.m.	time	12–1	1–3		1–2	12–1
	subject	Organisational Behaviour tutorial	Foundations of Marketing	free	Principles of Business tutorial	General tutorial
	room	Seminar room 2	Lecture room 3		Seminar room 1	Seminar room 2

Assignment 1.2

Student B

Student A has a complete weekly timetable. You will need to ask them questions so that you can complete your timetable.

		Monday	Tuesday	Wednesday	Thursday	Friday
a.m.	time	(1) _____	9–10	10–11	10–12	9–11
	subject	Organisational Behaviour	(3) _____	(5) _____	Principles of Business	(7) _____
	room	Main lecture hall	Language laboratory	Seminar room 1	(6) _____	Lecture room 2
p.m.	time	12–1	(4) _____		1–2	12–1
	subject	Organisational Behaviour tutorial	Foundations of Marketing	free	Principles of Business tutorial	(8) _____
	room	(2) _____	Lecture room 3		Seminar room 1	Seminar room 2

Assignment 1.3

Good learning styles quiz: key to your answers

1 Good learners try to contribute to classes and actively participate by sharing ideas and opinions. The best answer is B.

2 Good learners are well-prepared and organised. The best answer is A.

3 Good learners recognise that there may be more than one answer to a question. The best answer is B.

4 Good learners enjoy learning and care about their studies. The best answer is B.

5 Good learners sometimes become frustrated. It is a sign that they are trying to understand something. The best answer is A.

UNIT 3 Living space

Assignment 3.1

Flatmates quiz: key to your answers

1 A = 0, B = 2, C = 1, D = 4
2 A = 4, B = 2, C = 1, D = 0
3 A = 0, B = 1, C = 4, D = 2
4 A = 4, B = 0, C = 1, D = 2
5 A = 0, B = 1, C = 4, D = 2

0–7 points

You are a very private and independent person who prefers to have your own space. You would not like the kind of flatmate who has lots of visitors. You want other people to respect your privacy and your things.

8–14 points

You sometimes prefer to be alone, but you would like your flatmate to be good company and help with the housework. It's not a problem if they have visitors from time to time, and you might join in the fun.

15–20 points

You like to share and you need a flatmate who is friendly. You find it difficult to live alone or with a person who is shy and cool towards you. You are happy to do the housework together most of the time.

UNIT 6 Energy

Assignment 6.1

Student B

Student A has an incomplete set of notes about the Eden Project, and you have a complete set of notes. Answer Student A's questions to help them complete their notes.

The Eden Project

Opening days:	every day
Opening times:	9.30–4.30
Cost: Adult	£12.50
Student	£6.00
Group rate:	£35 for a group of 25
Tour length:	one hour

Assignment 6.2

Student A

Describe this diagram to Student B.

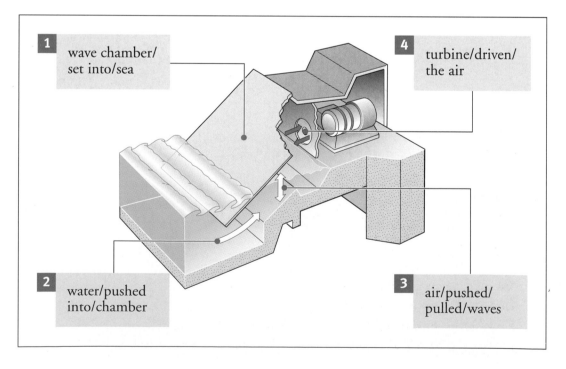

1 wave chamber/ set into/sea

4 turbine/driven/ the air

2 water/pushed into/chamber

3 air/pushed/ pulled/waves

UNIT 7 Cities

Assignment 7.1

Student A

Read out this description to Student B, who then has to guess which city it is.

This city has the same name as the country. It is in the south-east of Asia and is an island. It used to be a British colony. It is a commercial and trading city, and is one of the richest countries in the world. It has four official languages including Malay, English, Chinese and Tamil. It is one of the world's busiest ports, and I think it's one of the cleanest cities in the world.

Answer: Singapore

Assignment 7.2

Student B

Read out this description to Student A, who then has to guess which city it is.

This is in northern Europe in the east of the country. It is a capital city but it isn't the largest city. The main feature is a castle on a hill looking over the city. Europe's biggest festival of art and culture takes place here every August. It's an ancient and very beautiful city with lots of things for visitors to see and do.

Answer: Edinburgh

UNIT 8 Communication

Assignment 8.1

Writing quiz: key to your answers

If you scored more than 12, you are a thoughtful writer.
If you scored less than 8, you need to slow down and take care.
If you scored between 8, and 12 you can improve with more practice.

UNIT 9 Fitness and health

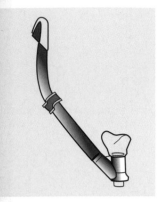

Assignment 9.1

Student A

Describe this object to Student B, who has to name the object. You could use descriptions such as:

- used in diving
- made of plastic and rubber
- used for breathing underwater
- put it between your teeth.

The object is a *snorkel*.

Assignment 9.2

Student A

You are the examiner, Student B is the candidate. Read the instructions to Student B.

I'm going to give you a topic, which I'd like you to talk about for one to two minutes. Before you start, you will have one minute to think about what you are going to say. You may make notes if you wish. Here is a pencil and some paper. I'd like you to talk about an activity you enjoy doing in your spare time.

UNIT 10 Charities

RAG week sponsored parachute jump

Date and time:
13 and 14 June at 2 p.m.

Place:
Airfield

Jump from a plane with an instructor from 3,000 metres.

Minimum age:
16-years-old

Assignment 10.1

Student A

Student B will ask you for details about a sponsored parachute jump. Answer their questions using the information.

UNIT 12 Academic success

Assignment 12.1

Learning types quiz: key to your answers

Mostly As

You are a visual learner; you learn by looking.

Mostly Bs

You are a auditory learner; you learn by listening.

Mostly Cs

You are a kinaesthetic learner; you learn by doing something.

IELTS and achieve IELTS

CD 1 Track 1

The International English Language testing system has two versions: academic and general training. The academic version is for students who would like to go to an English speaking university or college, whereas the general training version is for students who would like to take a training programme. I'll describe the academic version only here.

There are four parts to IELTS. These are listening, reading, writing and speaking, and they are taken in this order. Only the reading and writing modules are different for the general training and the academic versions of the test.

The listening test is in four sections, with ten questions for each section. The first two sections are about social life; the next two sections are based on educational or training situations. Students listen to talks by one person or conversations between two, three or four people. The listening section takes 40 minutes to complete.

The next section is the reading test. There are three texts or reading passages from a wide variety of sources including newspaper articles, books and magazines. Students need to answer 40 questions in one hour.

The third test is the writing test. The writing test has two tasks. In the first task students write about a chart or diagram, or write about a process, or describe an object or event. In the second part, among other things students could be asked to write about a problem or give their opinion about a subject. Students have one hour to complete the writing test. Usually students spend 20 minutes on task 1 and 40 on task 2.

The final test is the speaking test, which takes up to 14 minutes. The speaking test is an interview with three parts. In the first part the examiner and candidate introduce themselves. In the second part the student talks about a topic the examiner gives them. And finally, the candidate is given a general topic for discussion.

The International English Language testing system is often used by universities and colleges with courses given in English, to judge the level of students applying for their courses. At undergraduate level universities and colleges often look for students with an IELTS score of 5.5 and above, which means the student is a modest user of English and can understand the general message in most situations. The acceptance score varies and, of course, depends on the university or college.

UNIT 1: On course

CD 1 Track 2

Belen: I'm here to register for my course.

Registrar: OK, what's your surname?

Belen: Pérez.

Registrar: And how do you spell that?

Belen: P-É-R-E-Z.

Registrar: Sorry, could you repeat that please?

Belen: P-E-R …

Registrar: That's R for river.

Belen: Yes, that's right, then É-Z.

Registrar: Right, I think I've got that now. We don't want the wrong name on your student card. And your first name?

Belen: Belen.

Registrar: Is that with double L?

Belen: No, just one L.

Registrar: OK … Give me one moment to bring your details up on screen. There, I think I've got you. Now you're enrolled with the School of Management?

Belen: That's right.

Registrar: And the course is called International Business and Management Studies.

Belen: Yes.

Registrar: Now, let me just check the code for the course. I have it here as N100 BSc-BMS.

Belen: Could you say that again?

Registrar: Yes, course: code N100 BSc-BMS.

Belen: Yes, that's right.

Registrar: Now, I'll need to take a few more details before I can enrol you.

Belen: OK.

Registrar: Can you give me your address?

Belen: I'm in University hall – room 81, K floor.

Registrar: OK, and have you got a phone in your room?

Belen: Yes. It's not connected yet, but I know the number.

Registrar: And the number is?

Belen: 55046.

Registrar: Double five O four six. Great. And what's your date of birth?

Belen: I was born in 1986, on December 3.

Registrar: That's the third of December 1986.

Belen: That's correct.

Registrar: And finally, your marital status.

Belen: What's that?

Registrar: If you're married or single, or have a partner.

Belen: Oh no. I'm not married.

Registrar: So, single. That's all. Go to the next desk and have your photo taken for your student card. Your student number is UB 10984, and your e-mail address is perez@bradford.ac.uk

Belen: One minute, let me get a pen. bperez@bradford.ac.uk

Registrar: That's correct.

Belen: Thank you very much.

CD 1 Track 3

Could you repeat that please?

Could you say that again?

That's R for river.

Is that with double L?

No, just one L.

That's right. That's correct.

I think I've got that now.

Great.

CD 1 Track 4

Belen: Hi, there.

Tao: Hello.

Belen: Aren't you in the same hall as me?

Tao: I'm in University hall.

Belen: Yes, me too. We're both in the same hall. I thought I recognised you. We probably bumped into each other in the lift. My name's Belen.

Tao: I'm Tao.

Belen: Nice to meet you, Tao. We're probably taking similar subjects if we're here on the same day. Which department are you with?

Tao: I'm enrolled at the School of Management with the Department of Marketing.

Belen: I'm at the management school, too. What are you taking?

Tao: I'm doing Business and Marketing Studies.

Belen: Is that postgraduate or undergraduate?

Tao: It's a BSc – so I'm an undergraduate. What about you?

Belen: I'm also taking an undergraduate degree – a bachelor degree in International Business and Management with the Department of Business Studies.

Tao: Oh I looked at that course as well; it looks really interesting. Are you doing the four- or three-year course?

Belen: Me? I'm on the four-year course. What about you?

Tao: I'm still trying to decide. I really don't know what to do.

Belen: You're like me; it took me six months to decide which course to choose.

Tao: Well, we've certainly got something in common. How are we going to be business managers if we can't make decisions?!

Belen: But that's why we're here – to learn about decision-making.

Tao: I guess so. Are you picking up your timetable now?

Belen: Yes … we need to go to the department and see the course administrator.

Tao: Do you know where that is? With all the things to do – registration, Welcome packs, campus tours – I didn't have time to find out which room is the course administrator's.

Belen: It's on N floor.

Tao: N floor?

Belen: Let's go together. We can have a chat about the rooms and whether you should stay three or four years.

Tao: OK.

CD 1 Track 5

We're both in the same hall.

We're probably taking similar subjects.

I'm also taking an undergraduate degree.

We've certainly got something in common.

Aren't you in the same hall as me?

Yes, me too.

CD 1 Track 6

Examiner: How are you today?

Candidate: Very well thank you.

Examiner: And your name is ...?

Candidate: My name is Erzsébet.

Examiner: Could you spell that for me, please?

Candidate: It's E-R-Z-S-É with a dash above it -B-E-T, but you can call me Liz – it's easier.

Examiner: Can you tell me your candidate number?

Candidate: Yes, of course. It's 062266.

Examiner: How was your journey here?

Candidate: Not so good. The traffic is terrible in the city centre.

Examiner: Do you live far away?

Candidate: Not too far; about half an hour away.

CD 1 Track 7

My candidate number is 011 388.

My date of birth is 13th September 1985.

My address is 117 Horton Road.

Today's date is Wednesday 16th December.

My IELTS score is 5.5.

My home address is number 12 Richmond Road.

CD 1 Track 8

1   011 388
2   the 13th of September 1985
3   117 Horton Road
4   the 16th of December
5   5.5
6   12 Richmond Road

CD 1 Track 9

Belen: Hello. Are you the course administrator?

Administrator: Yes, I am. Please come in.

Belen: I'd like to get my timetable for term 1. Is it available yet?

Administrator: Yes, it is. There may be some changes at the start of term, but we'll let you know if there are and what they are. Now, can I take some details from you? What's your surname?

Belen: It's Peréz.

Administrator: Ah yes, I remember that name. You must be Belen. Welcome to the School of Management.

Belen: Thank you. I'm surprised you know who I am.

Administrator: It's my job to know all the students, where they are and how to contact them. We'll see each other quite often during your time here.

Belen: Oh good.

Administrator: So, you're taking International Business and Management.

Belen: That's right. I'm doing the four-year course.

Administrator: Now, your timetable. We'll give you a printed copy later, but for now I'll tell you what it is. Have you got a pen and paper handy?

Belen: Yes.

Administrator: You have lectures every morning. On Monday it's Languages for Business (French) from 10 to 12 in the language lab.

Belen: Sorry, where?

Administrator: In the language lab – language laboratory. Then on Tuesday …

Belen: Nothing else on Monday?

Administrator: No, the rest of Monday is free for studying. On Tuesday you start at 9 in the morning with Organisational Behaviour, level 1. Most first-year students need to attend this. That takes one hour until 10 and it's in the main lecture theatre. Then immediately after that you have a tutorial. In the afternoon you have another lecture from 2 to 3 – the Foundations of Marketing, level 1.

Belen: Foundations of Marketing, level 1. OK, what about Wednesday?

Administrator: On Wednesday in the morning you have the Foundations of Production from 9 to 11.

Belen: A two-hour lecture.

Administrator: Yes, Wednesday is a hard day. You have a one-hour tutorial immediately after that in seminar room 3. And we leave the afternoon free for sports and recreation; you don't have classes then.

Belen: So sports and recreation on Wednesday afternoon. What happens on Thursday?

Administrator: Thursday is also quite a busy day with a lecture on Information Systems in the morning, followed by tutorials from 11 to 12. Then you have a workshop from 12 to 1 in the main hall.

Belen: What's the workshop about?

Administrator: It's a workshop about study skills. One of the students from the School of Education is leading it. Then there is another lecture on Foundations of Global Economics in the afternoon in the main lecture theatre from 2 to 3.

Belen: Sorry, could you repeat that?

Administrator: Yes, of course. That's Thursday 2 – 3, main lecture theatre, the Foundations of Global Economics, and that's followed by a tutorial.

Belen: So, Thursday is quite a busy day.

Administrator: It is I'm afraid. But Friday is quieter; there's only one lecture. That's level 1, Environmental Issues in Business from 10 to 11 in the main lecture theatre, followed by Languages for Business (Japanese) – again in the language lab.

Belen: Well, that certainly is a lot of work.

Administrator: Yes, but you've always got the weekend to catch up on any work you haven't done.

Belen: Working at the weekend, too!

CD 1 Track 10

Person introducing seminar: Welcome to the seminar on study skills. In this session we're going to look at the characteristics of a good learner. Steven, you're leading the seminar today. Can you introduce yourself to the other students before you begin?

Steven: Yes ... as you heard, my name's Steven and I'm studying educational psychology. I'm in my third and final year. As part of my final year project I'm researching what makes a good learner – what characteristics do they have. If you have any questions, just stop me and ask. Studies show that people who are intelligent do not do as well as they could if they have bad study habits. The standard formula for working at university is that for every hour's class time, you should spend at least three hours studying on your own.

Student: So on a three-module course that's nine hours each week.

Steven: At least nine hours – minimum. These nine hours need to be divided into things to do before and after class. First of all, students need to take responsibility for their own learning. Next, make sure you attend classes. Classes help to organise information and your learning. Classes are where ideas and information are explained, and examples are given. Try to take an active part in these classes; don't sit there quietly waiting for the end of a class. Getting involved in the class, asking questions and taking part in discussions makes learning interesting and helps understanding of the subject.

Student: And what about before and after class?

Steven: I'm just coming to that. You have an advantage if you prepare for the class before it – and this is especially true for students whose first language is not English. If there is a reading list set for the class, make sure you have read the material. If there are notes available on the department's website, make sure you read them before the lecture and have one or two questions in your mind. After each class go over your notes, make sure you understand each point the tutor made and see if you can come up with your own examples. Try discussing the class with another student or even test each other from your notes. More importantly, prepare questions about any points you didn't understand or you would like to know more about. You can ask your tutor the questions later, or in a tutorial.

UNIT 2: Campus

CD 1 Track 11

A: Excuse me ... Can you tell me the way to the Students' Union?

B: Yes ... Follow the signs to the library, then turn right. The Students' Union is in the communal building.

A: How do you get to the art gallery?

B: Turn left and go past the Ashfield and Pemberton buildings. When you get to the library, turn left. Go past the bookshop and the art gallery is on your left.

A: Sorry, could you repeat that last sentence?

B: Yes, go straight past the bookshop, the art gallery is on your left.

A: Can you tell me where the refectory is?

B: Yes, it's here in the Richmond building – it's on F floor.

CD 1 Track 12

Catherine: Sorry, are you lost?

Sam: Yes, I'm trying to find the Richmond building.

Catherine: That's the big building at the other side of the university.

Sam: How do I get there?

Catherine: Are you a new student?

Sam: No, I'm here for an interview.

Catherine: Have you got a map?

Sam: I think so – in the information pack. Let me see. Here it is.

Catherine: Look, we're here at the Phoenix building. You go towards the Communal building ...

Sam: Which direction is the Communal building in?

Catherine: It's that building over there.

Sam: I see.

Catherine: So go across the park, but don't go across the grass – it can be slippery when it rains, until you reach the Communal building.

Sam: Isn't the Student's Union there?

Catherine: Yes, it is. Turn right there and with your back to the Student's Union go up the steps, to the library entrance.

Sam: Sorry, I didn't quite catch that. Can you say that again?

Catherine: Take the steps up to the entrance of the library.

Sam: Okay.

Catherine: Then turn left. Go past the Department of Peace Studies in the Pemberton building and cross the car park.

Sam: Sorry, did you say go left across the park?

Catherine: No, the car park. Then you walk up Richmond road for about 100 metres. When you get to the statue the entrance is in front of you.

Sam: Thanks.

Catherine: What are you applying for?

Sam: I'm hoping to do a course in Pharmacy – I'm going to the department of pharmacology.

Catherine: That's really interesting, my housemate is in her final year.

Sam: Really, what's her name in case I bump into her?

Catherine: She's called Francesca, but I doubt that you'll meet her – it's a big department. What's your name?

Sam: I'm Sam.

Catherine: Are you going to the department now?

Sam: No, I'm going to the international office to sign up for a tour of the campus.

Catherine: Well good luck. See you around.

Sam: Thanks again.

CD 1 Track 13

Sorry, could you repeat that last sentence?

Sorry, I didn't quite catch that.

Can you say that again?

Did you say go left across the park?

CD 1 Track 14

Where is the refectory?

How do I get to the art gallery?

Can you tell me the way to the Student's Union?

Which direction is the international office in?

CD 1 Track 15

A: Can you tell me about a place you really enjoyed studying at?

B: I'm going to tell you about the University of Sydney.

A: Oh yeah. OK.

B: Well I suppose the University of Sydney is the place I remember best, so I'll talk about that.

A: Oh really, why is that?

B: It's the oldest university in Australia; it's certainly one of the best. The tutors were very friendly and my classmates were very nice.

A: When was the university founded?

B: It was established in the 19th century, I think.

A: Why did you go there?

B: I thought it may be a nice place to spend summer learning English, and it's not too far from my home.

A: How many students studied with you?

B: It was quite a small class – there were only eight students in my class.

A: Did you get on with the other students?

B: Yes, we had a great time.

CD 1 Track 16

Graham: Hi everyone, and welcome to the campus tour of the University of Victoria. My name's Graham and I'm a third year student here studying Maths and Stats – that's mathematics and statistics. Let me tell you a little about the University of Victoria before we begin. The university proper began in 1964, and today we have 18,000 undergraduate and graduate students at the university. The university itself is built in and around a big circle called the ring road, which you can see in front of us.

We're standing here outside the Students' Union. In front of us we have the Clearihue building. To the right of Clearihue is the University Centre. Behind the University Centre is the David Strong building. To the left of Clearihue is the library and behind Clearihue is the Cornett building. Let me give you a brief guide to the facilities and departments in these buildings.

The University Centre is where the art gallery and museum are; we're really lucky to be able to go there and look at the exhibitions. There's also a student information centre and financial aid office where students can get help with their fees and find out about grants and so on. The main auditoriums are there and that's where many important ceremonies take place. Behind us in the Students' Union we have a lot of entertainment facilities: there's the student radio station CFUV, the student newspaper, a cinema and a nightclub. Unfortunately, we don't have the time to use them as often as we would like to.

To the left of the University Centre is the Clearihue building. This is the centre for our humanities programmes. We have student computing facilities there, and it's also where my department – that is, maths and statistics – is located. We also have languages and philosophy there. Let's cross over the ring road now and walk over to the David Strong building.

This is one of the main teaching centres of the university. Here we have classrooms, seminar rooms, lecture halls and auditoriums, so if you are accepted at the university, you'll spend some time in this building. Next to this is the Cornett building. The departments of geography, political science and sociology, among others, are located here. Are there any questions so far? OK, then let's walk across the park to the Centre for Medical Sciences and the Cunningham building.

CD 1 Track 17

Tutor: OK then, I'd like Lucas to begin the seminar by talking about technology in education and the virtual campus.

Lucas: Well, as part of my research project I've been looking into new technology in education. It's called VLE and that stands for virtual learning environment, or sometimes remote learning.

Student A: Sounds interesting.

Lucas: The ideas is to use computer networks to deliver information, lectures and reading materials to students. In effect students would learn from a distance, creating a virtual campus.

Tutor: But this isn't a new idea is it?

Lucas: No. Distance learning has a long history and many countries have an Open University. The university broadcasts programmes to students who work at home and may go to the university for a short period only – you know … do a short course in the summer.

Student B: So how is the virtual campus different from the Open University?

Lucas: Well, not every university can afford to make and broadcast TV programmes, for a start. But most universities have powerful computers on a network. This means that students could watch a live lecture on a webcam or a recorded lecture over the Internet. Instead of seminars like this, students can enter university chatrooms or virtual learning environments to talk to their tutor and other students. Video conferencing may replace tutorials for example.

Student C: But what about real interaction with the lecturers?

Lucas: Well if you think about it, there's not much interaction in lectures anyway. That is to say, students usually listen and take notes.

Tutor: Are there any other benefits to a virtual campus?

Lucas: Yes. First, there are two similar and opposite consequences. The number of students at university will drop as many decide not to go to a real lecture, but see the lecture online instead in their own time. At the same time the number of students will increase, as they don't have to leave home or travel a long way to go to university. So the number of real students at university will drop, but the number of virtual students will increase. Second, students will be able to choose to attend specific lectures and personalise their degree. What I mean by this is that students can decide which parts of the course are more relevant to what they want to do and take only these parts, not the whole course.

Student A: This sounds very exciting, but there must be some disadvantages.

Lucas: A possible disadvantage is that students could loose the social life at university.

Student C: What, like going to the Union bar and meeting in societies like the Film society?

Lucas: Yes, possibly. And meeting other students face to face.

Student B: And what about students who don't know how to use a computer?

Lucas: I'm afraid they need to learn. Nowadays you need to use computers in nearly all kinds of jobs. So, if you don't learn now, your chances of getting a job at the end of the course could be quite poor.

Tutor: How far have universities got with this?

Lucas: Well, a lot of universities deliver training over their computer networks already and the University of Sydney has started to offer business degrees online, so the virtual department is already here – it's probably only a matter of time before we have the virtual campus.

UNIT 3: Living space

CD 1 Track 18

Lily: Ahmed, Keiko! Hello. We're all at home at the same time! How unusual is that? Ahmed, how are you?

Ahmed: Not so good, actually. I've got three assignments to do before the end of the month. One of them is late already. I'm so worried about my writing. My tutor has told me she can't understand what I mean, because my grammar is so bad.

Keiko: Don't worry, Ahmed. I'll help you with that. I got top marks for grammar on the Foundation course. Lily, are you making a cup of tea?

Lily: Yes. Would you like one? Ahmed?

Ahmed: Yes, please.

Lily: And there's something I want to talk to you about, now we're all together. Well, it's my birthday next week and I'd like to have a party here, in our house. Is that all right with you?

Keiko: Yes, excellent idea.

Lily: And will you help me with the preparations?

Ahmed: Of course.

Lily: I made a list. There are quite a lot of things to do. First of all, there's the shopping. I know what to buy, and I'll pay for it, but I need someone to come to the supermarket with me to help me pack, and get the stuff in the taxi.

Ahmed: When are you going to go?

Lily: After classes next Wednesday. I thought we could make spaghetti with salad. I'm going to ask people to bring their own drinks, but I'll also buy some soft drinks and juice.

Ahmed: I won't be able to help you, I'm afraid. I agreed to help at the Students' Union with the preparations for the dance this weekend.

Keiko: It's all right. I'll go with you.

Lili: Thanks, Keiko. We also need to make the place look nice when people come here – not like it is now. Will you help me with this?

Ahmed: Yes, I suppose so.

Lily: Good. Here's list of things to do. The bathroom first – we'll clean the toilet and the bath. Then there's the kitchen. Everything has to be ready and all the washing-up finished. Will you both make sure the living room's tidy, too?

Keiko: That's a lot of work. I'll do the kitchen. I'll do the washing-up first, then clean the floor. Ahmed, will you do the bathroom?

Ahmed: Ugh. All right, I'll clean the toilet and the bath.

Lily: Thanks, Ahmed. I'll do the living room. I'll vacuum the carpet and move the chairs and tables.

Keiko: Now let's check that we all know what we're going to do. I'm going to do the washing-up and clean the kitchen floor. What are you going to do, Ahmed?

Ahmed: I'm going to clean the bathroom. Lily's going to vacuum the carpet in the living room, and move the chairs and tables in.

Lily: Good! Let's get started. It won't take very long.

CD 1 Track 19

Lily: That was a great party, but look at the state of this place. Who spilt a drink on the floor? It's made a terrible mess. We're going to be in trouble when the landlord sees that. He's coming to collect the rent today, so we have to tidy up, and soon.

Ahmed: Well, it wasn't me. I stayed in the kitchen most of the time. I was talking to Betty about the Students' Union dance last Saturday.

Keiko: It wasn't me either. I bet it was that guy with the guitar. He was sitting there most of the time. I think he's a psychology student in the first year. Who invited him?

Lily: Not me.

Keiko: Well I didn't speak to him. So who's responsible for the mess? Whoever it is should clean it up.

Lily: I think we are all. We all invited friends and so we should share the cleaning up. There are glasses and plates to wash, all this rubbish needs throwing away and the bottles taking to the recycling centre. We also need to clean up the stain on the floor. And have you seen the kitchen today? It's an absolute tip. Why did we decide to cook spaghetti? Someone spilled sauce all over the floor.

Ahmed: I've got a terrible headache. I think I'll go back to bed for a while. Have either of you got any aspirins?

Keiko: Oh, Ahmed. You always try to get out of doing the housework. When was the last time you washed up, or cooked a meal for us?

Ahmed: I can't cook. My mum always did the cooking. She did the washing-up, too. In fact, she did everything in the house. She never asked me or my brothers to help, and of course she never asked my father.

Lily: But your mum isn't here now, so you must do some things for yourself. You can start with the living room. Here's a bag. Put all the rubbish in it, and put the bottles in a box in the kitchen. When you're finished you have to take the bottles for recycling. Keiko, do you have any ideas about that stain on the floor?

Keiko: I'll get the scrubbing brush and try to clean it up. I don't think it will come out completely, though. I could look on the Internet for help. I think there is a website from that programme on the television about keeping your house clean.

Lily: OK, I'll vacuum the floor when you're finished, and I suppose that means I'll do the washing-up as well. I'm not doing the whole kitchen by myself though. Ahmed can clean the floor. Where is he? Ahmed … Ahmed!

CD 1 Track 20

Look at the state of this place.
What a mess.
It's so untidy.
It's an absolute tip.

CD 1 Track 21

Irona: Welcome to the university. My name is Irona Dougherty, and together with my assistant, Pat Wesley, we look after all the accommodation on campus. There are halls of residence on both campuses, and this is where you will stay for at least the first six months of your course. As many of you are from overseas, you will be safer and more secure living on campus until you get to know the town and the way people do things in this country.

Each hall has a shared kitchen, with lockable cupboards for each resident. Some of the rooms have their own shower and fridge. Of course, these rooms are a little more expensive. Others have shared bathrooms on each floor. If you prefer not to share accommodation with the opposite sex, we have two single-sex halls. The others are mixed. You may have a personal phone and TV in your room if you wish. But remember that, in this country, you must buy a licence for your television.

This campus is very safe, we have 24-hour security staff on call. You can contact them on 07982 694837 at any time. If you lose your key, they have access to all the rooms. Your mail will be delivered to the porter's lodge. That is in the central building, where the canteen and the Students' Union are. The porters are very friendly; they will soon know you by name and have your mail ready for you when you walk in the door. When you need to do your washing, there are two laundrettes – one on each campus. There are washing machines and driers in each of them, and you can iron your clothes there too.

Another advantage of living on campus is that the housekeeping staff will provide you with clean sheets every week, and clean the kitchen and bathrooms every day. We also have a caretaker, John Hawes, who will come and fix anything that is broken in the halls. The best way to contact him is through the main receptionist. Just dial zero on any of the internal phones around the university.

After the first six months, you may decide you want to rent a place privately. There is a range of accommodation available in the town. The cheapest of these are bedsits – that's a self-contained room that you use for sleeping, studying and relaxing. You will normally have to share a kitchen and bathroom. There are also some apartments available, if you want to be more private. Most of these have only one bedroom, and they can be quite expensive. The other option is to move into a shared house. Many of our students do this in the second year. Check the noticeboard in the Accommodation office if you are looking for a room in a shared house.

Right, well … I think that's everything. Any questions? No? Well I'm sure you'll have plenty later on! I'll see you all at two o'clock this afternoon for coffee and biscuits, and a tour of the campus. Please meet me in the foyer, which is on the first floor of this building. It's the big room with lots of chairs, and magazines and newspapers. If you get lost, ask anyone you see downstairs. Thank you very much.

CD 1 Track 22

messy
cosy
gloomy
tidy
stuffy
airy

CD 1 Track 23

Let me tell you about my home. We live in a new development on the edge of the city, about an hour away from here. I live in a medium-size apartment with my parents. It's just right for a small family – it's modern and comfortable. When you enter our flat there's a small room for coats. The next room is the living and dining room – we don't have separate rooms for this. We're a bit untidy and it's always a little messy there. The kitchen is next to this. The kitchen is quite cramped, but we have a balcony where we can sit outside in good weather. As you go from the living room into the corridor, on the right are the bedrooms, and the bathroom is at the end of the corridor, on the left.

UNIT 4: Film society

CD 1 Track 24

Tao: Hi, Catherine.

Catherine: Hello, Tao. What are you up to?

Tao: I'm off to the Students' Union first to get some paper for my printer, then I'm going to the students' cinema to catch a film.

Catherine: Oh really? What's on?

Tao: There are a couple of films I'm interested in. There's *City of God* ...

Catherine: What's that about?

Tao: It's a true story about gangs in the poorest part of a city in Brazil.

Catherine: Uh huh. And?

Tao: And *Touching the Void*. It's a dramatisation about two mountain climbers – Joe Simpson and Simon Yates.

Catherine: That sounds a bit boring.

Tao: Oh no, not at all – it's really exciting. It's a docudrama about a climb in the Andes, and how a climber survived a disastrous fall.

Catherine: What's a docudrama?

Tao: It's part documentary and part drama.

Catherine: Oh really! What time does it begin?

Tao: The cinema opens at 7.30, but there are usually 15 minutes of trailers and advertisements, so it will begin at about 7.45.

Catherine: That's quarter to eight. And how long does it last?

Tao: It's just over an hour and a half.

Catherine: How much is it to get in?

Tao: Well, because it's at the students' cinema it's cheaper than the cineplex. If you show your student card, then you can get a student discount of 25 per cent.

Catherine: Oh that's good.

Tao: And if you are a member of the Film society ...

Catherine: What's that?

Tao: It's like a club that organises films and helps to run the students' cinema.

Catherine: I see.

Tao: Then you get a further 25 per cent discount, so you could get in at half the price – that's £2.25, instead of £4.50.

Catherine: Are you in the Film society, Tao?

Tao: Yes.

Catherine: What kind of reviews did *Touching the Void* get?

Tao: It got excellent reviews in the newspaper and on TV ... five stars in fact. But I'm going because our tutor recommended it.

Catherine: Oh, really? Then it must be good. How long is it on for?

Tao: It finishes today. So, if you want to see it you'd better come with me.

Catherine: Why not ... I think I'll enjoy it.

Tao: How good was that?

Catherine: I really enjoyed it – it's a great film. You can hardly believe they survived.

Tao: Which bit did you like the best?

Catherine: There were lots of parts I liked: I thought the part at the beginning was really good when they were climbing the mountain really quickly. I also liked the part where they were sleeping at the camp when they heard Joe calling. But I think the bit I liked best was when the climbers were telling their story to the camera. Their adventure was so incredible. I just enjoyed listening to them. Which part did you like?

Tao: The part of the film that impressed me? When Joe broke his leg and Simon was lowering him down the mountain on a rope.

Catherine: Uh huh.

Tao: And then Simon lowered Joe over the edge of the mountain.

Catherine: By mistake of course, and Joe was hanging over the mountain edge on the rope trying to climb back up.

Tao: But his fingers were frozen, so he couldn't do anything.

Catherine: And then what Simon did next ... what a choice to make.

Tao: That caused big arguments in the climbing community.

Catherine: I bet it did.

CD 1 Track 25

It's really exciting.
How good was that?
I really enjoyed it – it's a great film.

CD 1 Track 26

Sara: Hi, everyone. Sorry I'm late.

Barbara: Hi, Sara. Glad you could make it; we're talking about event organisation today. We're just starting so take a seat. So, on the agenda today we have apologies, minutes of the last meeting, and two items: the quality of the films at the students' cinema, and the Film society end-of-term party. Finally, we have any other business. So ... apologies: Shin can't be here because he needs to finish an assignment and unfortunately Tao can't be here either – he's ill. So, James, can you take the minutes of the meeting?

James: Me?

Barbara: Yes, just take notes about what we say and I'll help you to type them up later.

James: Well, I'll give it a go.

Barbara: Now, did everyone read the minutes of the last meeting?

All: Yes.

Barbara: And are there any comments or objections? No? So, James, minutes of last meeting are approved with no objections.

James: Minutes approved.

Barbara: There are two items today: the state of our equipment and to organise our annual film event – film night. Let's move on to the first item on the agenda – and that's from Istvan. Istvan, can you tell us a bit more about it?

CD 1 Track 27

Istvan: Let me introduce myself to new members. I'm the Film society projectionist. Over the past few weeks there have been some complaints about the quality of the films at the students' cinema. I checked with the film distributors and they said that the quality of the film they sent was absolutely fine. So I cleaned the projector and looked for any worn or bad parts, but I couldn't see anything wrong there. Finally I checked the screen. And here's the bad news.

James: I hope you're not going to ask for any money.

Istvan: We need a new screen.

James: [Groan.]

Istvan: The screen we have at the moment is badly marked. It's dirty and it's yellowing – becoming yellow with age. This means that when I project a film onto it the colour is not as good as it should be, and people notice this.

Barbara: OK, when do we need to replace it and how much is it going to cost?

Istvan: If we're lucky we can use the old one until the end of this term – that's only three more films. As for the cost – we're looking at about £1,500.

James: [Chokes.]

Barbara: Take it easy, James. How much have we got in the bank?

James : The society has £50 in the current account, £200 in the deposit account and in cash – let me see – £5.50.

Sara: So we've got a bit of a problem.

James: Just a bit.

Barbara: Let's see. We need to raise about £1,300 before term begins again in September.

James: That's right.

Barbara: Any suggestions anyone?

Sara: Sorry to interrupt, but could we move on to the next item on the agenda – it may help with our problem.

CD 1 Track 28

Barbara: Secretary, what's the next item? [Pause.] James, you're the secretary today – remember?

James: Oh yes. The next item is the Film society's annual party.

Barbara: Sara, your thoughts on this.

Sara: Well, for the Film society's party I'm planning to have a theme night – thriller night, or horror night or …

Istvan: Hungarian film night.

Sara: Er … or something like that, and to show films all through the night from 9 pm to 9 am. So any suggestions about the theme would be great.

James: How about a Jackie Chan night, or a martial arts night?

Istvan: Or a Hungarian film night?

Sara: I was thinking about a Star Wars night and asking everyone to come dressed as a character from the films.

Barbara: That's a good idea. Can we ask members to put in their suggestions at the next meeting and I'd like to suggest having a vote on the best theme. So, James, minute that under 'Chair's action'. I have to organise and arrange a vote on the theme for the film night. Now, Sara, back to the screen.

Sara: I think that during the film night we can have special fund-raising events.

James: Like?

Sara: Like, for example, a film quiz, or a raffle or a competition for the best costume.

Barbara: That's a great idea, especially the costume competition. How many Star Wars films are there now?

Istvan: There were five when I last counted.

Barbara: So that's about ten film hours with fund-raining events in between. Sara, what's the position with the Students' Union?

Sara: We've got the union for the 23 May, and they will keep the bar open for food and drink until 1.30. After this there will be a drinks machine in the cinema and I'll open the snack bar for food.

Barbara: How much do you think we can raise from this?

James: I don't think we can get £1,300 from just one night, to be frank.

Sara: But it will give us a good start.

Barbara: I agree with you both; I think we need more ideas.

Istvan: We could ask for a bigger budget from the Students' Union for the next year.

Barbara: I'd like to avoid doing that. Traditionally we're one of the few societies that makes money for the Union. I don't want to go to the Sports and Societies president asking for money. Now, come on, we can do this ourselves. Any more suggestions?

James: How about putting up the price of the tickets by £1? That will give us an extra £100 each film, and with three films before the end of term, that gives us £300.

Barbara: That's a very serious proposal. We need to have a vote on this. Members in favour of increasing the ticket price raise your hands now please. Those against?

CD 1 Track 29

Now for the fund-raising event.
Any more suggestions anybody?
I'd like to suggest a charity walk.
Isn't that a bit boring?
Let's do something fun.
How about climbing the Senate house?
I think we should avoid doing that.
We don't want to get into trouble.

CD 1 Track 30

My favourite film is the Matrix because it's such a fast-moving film. It's a science fiction film but at the same time you could call it an action film. I saw it a few years ago as soon as it was released, in fact I was the first one of my friends to see it. The best part of the film was when the main character was trying to rescue his friend. I like this part because the special effects are amazing. It made a big impression on me as it was technically so far ahead of any other film at that time – I liked it very much.

CD 1 Track 31

The centre of the film industry is Hollywood in America, which makes by far the largest amount of money. However, Hollywood isn't the biggest producer of films. In fact this is India, which produced over 700 films in 1999. The second largest producer is the USA, which made slightly over half the amount made in India at almost 400 films. In third position is Japan, which made nearly 300 films in 1999. The next largest producer of films was Italy, which made just over 100 films, although today Britain may have overtaken Italy in film production.

UNIT 5: Bulletin

CD 1 Track 32

Carmen: Hi, Paul. Come in and take a seat.

Paul: Oh OK, thanks.

Carmen: So welcome to CUe FM – the radio of the University of Canberra. Have you heard any of our output at all?

Paul: Oh sure, I listen to it most days.

Carmen: And which is your favourite programme?

Paul: I always try to catch the phone-in, but usually the radio is on in the background.

Carmen: Uh huh. Which department are you in?

Paul: I'm studying IMC.

Carmen: What's that?

Paul: IMC is Imaging and Media Communications.

Carmen: Oh, you're a technical person. We always need technical support. Are you interested in the technical side or are you interested in DJing?

Paul: I was really thinking about DJing – getting my own slot.

Carmen: Great, well let's get some details. What's your full name, Paul?

Paul: Paul Dyson.

Carmen: How long have you been at the university?

Paul: I've been here for nearly five months.

Carmen: So you know your way around pretty well by now.

Paul: I think so, but the university is so big – there's always something new.

Carmen: Now, what's your UCU number?

Paul: My University of Canberra number is … let me just get my card … I've put it in a safe place after I lost it yesterday! Here it is: UC double O five seven nine.

Carmen: Now before I tell you about CUe FM, why don't you tell me something about yourself … Why do you want to be a DJ?

Paul: Well, I've always been interested in music and I've always wanted to have a go at DJing. Also I've recently become interested in storing music electronically and I've done a lot of work on this in the department.

Carmen: Well as you probably know, we've got most of our music library on computer so it makes DJing a lot easier. Have you ever done DJing?

Paul: No, not really. I've done technical support for my old college radio station, but I've never been a DJ – although I've watched other people do it.

Carmen: So you're familiar with radio. What kind of music are you interested in?

Paul: I love world music and I've built a good collection of music from around the world.

Carmen: And you wouldn't mind sharing this with us?

Paul: No, that's really why I'd like to do a programme; I'd like to share my collection with other students.

Carmen: Oh sorry, have to stop you for a minute. What's up Ahmed?

Ahmed: Just got some news in from the women's rugby match.

Carmen: What's that?

Ahmed: Not good – we've lost.

Carmen: Again? What was the score?

Ahmed: 24 – 3 to Brisbane.

Carmen: We haven't just lost – we've been hammered. Quick – get it on to the newsdesk for the mid-afternoon news.

Ahmed: OK.

Carmen: 24 – 3. Huh. Well, you sound like you're right for the job. In a minute we'll give you a sound test to see how you sound on air. Before that, let me tell you a bit about the timetable. As you know we broadcast 24 hours a day, seven days a week.

Paul: Uh huh.

Carmen: This gives us 16 hours of live broadcasting, usually divided into four four-hour slots, depending on how many DJs we can organise. Every day we have the breakfast slot. This is usually a mix of pop and rock songs with news items and chat.

Paul: What kind of news do you broadcast?

Carmen: Oh, local news usually about the university, events, student sports, new jobs and appointments – that kind of thing. Then we have the mid-afternoon slot – we usually keep that music, competitions and news. And after that is the evening set; we have a wide variety of things then – competitions, news and reviews of concerts at the university, shows in the city and so on. There is some music, but it tends to be more like a talk show. The late show is mostly music with some phone-in slots. We also give out the results of the competitions then.

Paul: So where would I fit in then?

CD 1 Track 33

… tell me something about yourself.

Well as you probably know …

let me tell you a bit about …

CD 1 Track 34

Newscaster: Good evening and welcome to the 6 o'clock news. It's Thursday the 3rd of April, and now the world news headlines.

Scientists have found what could be another planet orbiting around the sun. The discovery was made by an American team of scientists led by Mike Brown. The object is nearly as big as Pluto but is three times further away than the most distant known planet and takes an incredible 12,000 years to orbit the Sun. The planet is redder than any other object in the solar system apart from Mars. Scientists have named the object Sedna after the Inuit goddess of the ocean. It is the most distant object so far discovered in our solar system and the largest object discovered since scientists found Pluto in 1930. The discovery has caused discussion among astronomers about exactly what is a planet. Some have said the new object is, in fact, a comet; others, like the team of scientists that found it, have called Sedna a planetoid – or small planet.

South Korea has become the fifth country with a high-speed railway after Japan, France, Germany and Spain with the launch of the KTX or Korean Train Express. The French-designed KTX completed the journey in just two hours and 40 minutes. It previously took at least four hours. The project has cost US$15.3 billion, and was developed over 12 years. Officials hope that the new service will help South Korea's crowded roads. With an average speed of 300 kilometres per hour, the KTX will carry 180,000 passengers a day, allowing the Korean National Railway to cut back on slower services and boost freight transport. At an opening ceremony earlier in the week, the South Korean President said the KTX would be linked to the inter-Korean railway, the Trans-Siberian railway and the Trans-China railway.

Business news now … and another music company, EMI, has cut 1,500 jobs and dropped one in five of its artists in the latest cost-cutting exercise in the music business. EMI, whose performers include the Rolling Stones and Robbie Williams, has a worldwide workforce of 8,000 people and is the world's third largest music company. Previously, Universal Music Group, the world's largest music company, announced it planned to cut 1,300 jobs, saying that this was due to Internet piracy. EMI said that the cost cuts could save £50 million. Since 2001 EMI has cut 1,900 jobs and 400 artists – including Mariah Carey, whose contract was cancelled two years ago at a cost of £38 million.

As we have been on air we have been receiving news of an upset in the presidential elections in America. More on that story later as details come in …

CD 1 Track 35

Lecturer: OK everyone, you've been here for a few months now listening to me talking in seminars – now it's over to you. I asked everyone to prepare a short talk about information and communications in the 21st century today and I gave you a list of topics I wanted you to cover. So I hope you're all ready. After each person has spoken there will be time for a discussion about the issues raised in the talk. So who's first? Paula?

Paula: Yes, OK. Er … well my name's Paula and I'm going to give a brief talk about news broadcasting. I'm going to start by looking at an example of a national news broadcaster, and talk about where they get their news from and how they select which news items to broadcast. Then I'll take a short look at press agencies and associations, and go into the differences between them. For each type I'll give an example so that it's clear what I mean.

Lecturer: Sounds good.

Paula: Large organisations like the BBC in the UK and the New York Times in the USA usually have their own newsgathering networks and will syndicate or sell their stories to other organisations.

The BBC is the world's largest newsgathering operation with 41 international offices. However, not every organisation is big enough to employ journalists all around the world, so smaller organisations buy news from press agencies and press associations. Even large news organisations use these agencies when they gather news.

Let's move on to examine press agencies and associations.

Press agencies are organisations established to supply news to newspapers, magazines, and radio and television broadcasters. They generally prepare articles that can be used by other news organisations. They provide these articles electronically. Originally they used telegraphs; today they frequently use the Internet. Corporations, individuals and intelligence agencies often also use press agencies as sources of information. Press agencies can be either corporations that sell news, co-operatives composed of newspapers that share their articles with each other, or government agencies.

Let me have a quick drink of water. … That's better. So, now I'll go on to co-operative press agencies.

Gathering news is an expensive business, so many co-operative agencies were formed by newspapers who wanted to save costs by sharing their news. The oldest co-operative press agency in America is the Associated Press, formed in 1848 by six New York newspapers. In Asia an important agency is Kyodo, which is a non-profit making organisation. Kyodo is a Japanese agency, which was formed in 1945. It gets its money from membership payments and subscribers, and has about 1,000 journalists working for it.

Another kind of press agency is the corporate press agency. These make money by selling news. An example of this is Reuters – one of the world's largest suppliers of news. Reuters was set up in 1851 and now has 2,000 journalists working all over the world.

Finally, we have government press agencies. A good example of these is the Russian press agency, ITAR-TASS. Originally called TASS, which stood for Telegraph Agency of the Soviet Union, it was established in 1925 and run by the Communist Party. By the late 1980s it is estimated that TASS employed about 65,000 journalists.

Let's take a look now at the advantages and disadvantages of each type of press agency …

UNIT 6: Energy

CD 1 Track 36

Sara: Hi, Catherine.

Catherine: Hi.

Sara: Are you planning a trip for the Easter holiday?

Catherine: No, no time for that.

Sara: So what are all those brochures you've got?

Catherine: Oh, these.

Sara: Yes, let me see: Snowdon National Park offices, Dinorwig Electric Mountain, the Centre for Alternative Technology, the National Botanic Gardens in Carmarthenshire …

Catherine: Uh huh.

Sara: I thought you wanted to go to Spain during the holidays. When did you change your plan? Are you sure you want to spend your holidays at these places?

Catherine: I've told you, it's not a holiday.

Sara: Well what is it?

Catherine: It's a field trip … you know, research – something you Arts students don't do.

Sara: Excuse me – I spent Christmas in Glasgow studying Rennie Mackintosh and Art Nouveau.

Catherine: I mean real research; not just looking at things.

Sara: So what exactly do you mean by real research, if it's not just looking at things, as you put it?

Catherine: We've been given a project by our tutor into sustainable energy development in an area of the UK. She put us into groups and gave us each an area to report on.

Sara: How many words?

Catherine: Don't ask. We've got to hand in a report of 2,500 words and lead a seminar of 20 minutes. So that means we'll need to show slides and prepare handouts for the other students.

Sara: And when's the deadline?

Catherine: The tutor set the deadline for the second week after the break – so mid-May.

Sara: So, in fact it's not that you want to do field work instead of going to Spain, you have to do it!

Catherine: I suppose you could put it that way.

Sara: Where are you going then?

Catherine: We split our group into three areas: north and mid-Wales; south-west Wales; and south-east Wales. I'm covering north and mid-Wales; I'm going with Shin.

Sara: But he doesn't do engineering.

Catherine: No, but he's at a loose end during the break and he wanted to tag along.

Sara: I see. So he's got some time on his hands. When are you starting?

Catherine: We'll go to Snowdon next Thursday and visit the National Park offices there the next day.

Sara: Why are you going there?

Catherine: They're a good example of offices that are designed to be energy saving with low energy lighting and good insulation. I think we'll spend the weekend there in the National Park … perhaps do a bit of walking.

Sara: I've been told that it's an amazingly beautiful part of the country.

Catherine: Yes, me too. After that we'll go down over to Dinorwig to see an example of a hydroelectric power station.

Sara: But why is that so special?

Catherine: The power station is actually built inside the mountain.

Sara: Really. That sounds fascinating.

Catherine: I'm trying to get a guided tour of that. We'll stay overnight near there at Caernarfon and the next morning head off to Machynlleth to look at the Centre for Alternative Technology.

Sara: Right.

Catherine: You can stay there as part of a residential visit, so I'm trying to organise the rest of our team to meet there and stay one or two nights.

Sara: That's great.

Catherine: Then on Thursday we'll head back here and start to prepare our presentation.

Sara: So that gives you ten days' preparation time.

Catherine: Yes; I hope it's enough.

CD 1 Track 37

he's at a loose end
he wanted to tag along
he's got some time on his hands

CD 1 Track 38

Answer machine: Hello, this is the Electric Mountain Visitor Centre. To hear our opening times, press 1. To speak to an information officer, please hold the line.

Officer: Hello, Electric Mountain Visitor Centre.

Catherine: Hello, I'd like to arrange a visit to the centre and I wonder if you could give me some information about it.

Officer: Sure. To start with we're open every day from May to October; then from November to March it's five days a week.

Catherine: I'll be coming in May.

Officer: Then you need to know the opening times. In May we open at 10.30 in the morning and close at 4.30. Are you staying near the visitor centre?

Catherine: We're staying at Caernarfon.

Officer: Then you're not too far away. The tour takes two hours, so that's 11, 1 and 3 to catch a tour.

Catherine: Can you tell me what the tour includes?

Officer: Let me give you a quick description. There are three parts to the tour: some at the Electric Mountain Visitor Centre and some of it at the power station itself.

Catherine: OK.

Officer: The tour starts with a multi-media sound and vision show here, at Electric Mountain. From here, a tour bus will transport you underground to the power station for a guided tour of the power station. From the main gallery, you can see Dinorwig's massive generators in action.

Catherine: Could you tell me what Dinorwig is?

Officer: That's the name of the mountain where the power station is. In the gallery we show you a film that explains the building and commissioning of the power station. Then the bus takes you up to the surface and back to the Electric Mountain Visitor Centre.

Catherine: And that takes two hours?

Officer: That's right.

Catherine: And how much does it cost?

Officer: Are you part of a group or a student?

Catherine: I'm a student.

Officer: Well, we have a special discounted rate for students – the full price for an adult is £6, but for students it's £4.50.

Catherine: What about for groups? The tour sounds really interesting; so maybe I could get more people to come.

Officer: The minimum number of people per group is 20 and we have special rates for this.

Catherine: Would you mind telling me the group rate?

Officer: Of course not; it's £70 per group.

Catherine: OK, well I'll get back to you later.

Officer: You're very welcome. Bye.

CD 1 Track 39

Amarina: Welcome to the Centre for Sustainable Energy. My name is Amarina and I'm a research assistant at the centre. Let me tell you a little about us. We're a member of the School of Energy Sciences, which in turn is part of the Department of Engineering. We share the faculty with another department – IT (that's information technology) – and together we form the faculty of engineering and information technology. We were established in 1980 when several research groups with interests in the same area – that is, sustainable energy – came together to form the centre. Now altogether we have about 30 staff and research students, and our work covers everything from basic research and development to commercial research. In fact, the last area is very important to us as a centre as we get 80 per cent of our income from commercial research. Altogether we have a turnover of about US$2 million – but unfortunately that's not all profit. Now, that's enough for the introduction to the centre. I'll tell you a little bit about the facilities here as we walk around the centre. First of all we have the reception area, and here's our wonderful receptionist, Simon, to take any calls and deal with questions from outside.

Simon: Hello.

Amarina: Opposite him is the centre's administrator – Sungwoo Jeong, from Korea. Sungwoo deals with applications from students who want to join the centre and makes sure that everyone knows when their deadlines are. Let's go into the department proper. As you know, we are a research university and many of our facilities are devoted to R and D – research and development. So as you can see down the right-hand side of the corridor are our labs – research laboratories, that is.

Student: What are your primary research interests?

Amarina: As you know, we're the Centre for Sustainable Energy, so we're trying to develop and improve alternative ways of producing energy. Now, as we all know, what we have a lot of in Australia is sun. So as you will guess, most of our research is towards developing better and more efficient ways of producing solar energy.

Student: What kinds of things have you developed?

Amarina: Well that's a difficult question … not because the answer's difficult, but because there's so much to talk about. Let me give you a small example – one reason solar energy can be so expensive is because of the cost of the materials needed to build it. At the centre we found a way of producing the same material at a fraction of the previous cost. Now, on the left-hand side of the corridor are the research assistants' offices; they are the first two doors. Then we have a seminar room and after that a lecture room. That's where I spend most of my days – and nights, too, sometimes. The lecture room has all the latest equipment. And finally the last room on this corridor is Professor Karl Micova's office.

CD 1 Track 40

Lecturer: Hello, and good afternoon everyone. Today I'm going to talk about a source of renewable energy that we in the department have been researching and developing – solar energy. Why is this important? Well, the basic problem is very simple: we have a limited amount of fuels such as oil and other fossil fuels, and we need to find alternative ways of replacing these. There is, of course, another problem – using fossil fuels is changing the earth's climate and we simply don't know the consequence of this. We believe that solar energy can completely replace fossil and nuclear fuels over the next 50 years and today I'm going to tell you how. In fact the use of wind and solar power for energy production has increased by 25 per cent over the last ten years.

Solar energy is radiation produced by nuclear fusion reactions deep within the sun. The sun provides all the heat and light Earth receives and thus keeps every living being alive. Solar energy travels to Earth in what can be described as packets of energy called photons. The side of Earth facing the sun, which is just a square kilometre at the outer edge of our atmosphere, receives 1,400 megawatts of solar power every minute. However, only half of that reaches the Earth's surface. Clouds and the atmosphere absorb and scatter the other half of the sunlight. The light that reaches the ground depends on the time of the day, the day of the year and the amount of cloud.

As well as using the Sun for energy directly, we can use solar energy indirectly from three other sources. We can make use of solar energy that has been naturally collected in the Earth's atmosphere, oceans, and plant life, for example, we can get energy from the wind, the waves or from biomass and use this for power. To give you an example, the Sun's energy, working with the atmosphere and the oceans, produces winds that have turned windmills and driven sailing ships for centuries.

In recent years, people have invented two main types of solar energy collectors to capture and use direct solar energy: flat plate collectors and concentrating collectors. Both need large surface areas exposed to the Sun since so little of the Sun's energy reaches Earth's surface. Even in areas that receive a lot of sunshine, a large flat plate collector surface is needed to gather the energy that one person typically uses during a day.

Flat plate collectors are flat, thin boxes with a transparent cover that are put on rooftops facing the Sun. The Sun heats a black metal plate inside the box, this black plate is called an absorber plate, that transfers the heat from the Sun to a fluid, like water, for example running through tubes within the collector. The energy transferred to the tubes, is called the collector efficiency. Flat plate collectors can heat the carrier fluid up to 82°C or180°F. Their efficiency in making use of the available energy varies between 40 and 80 percent, depending on the type of collector.

After water has been heated by the flat plate collector it is sent to a circulating pump. The pump has a thermometer or a temperature sensor to control the temperature of the water and, if necessary, add cold water to keep the temperature at a reasonable level. Automatic controllers turn the circulation pump on when someone turns on a tap, and a storage tank keeps any extra water hot until it is required for use. That's the large tank you can see in the roof of the house.

UNIT 7: Cities

CD 1 Track 41

Paul: So whereabouts in Japan are you from Keiko?

Keiko: I'm from a suburb of Tokyo.

Paul: It must be a big change coming here.

Keiko: Yes, it's much less crowded here than back home. Tokyo's very overcrowded.

Paul: I can't remember which city is bigger – Hong Kong or Tokyo. Which is it?

Keiko: Tokyo is the biggest city in the world.

Paul: How many people live there?

Keiko: Over 12 million.

Paul: 12 million people! That's incredible. Is it more spacious than Sydney, too?

Keiko: No, it's just over 2,000 square kilometres in size.

Paul: That's a lot of people for that area.

Keiko: Can you imagine what rush hour is like? Our metro system is better than here, but it's still pretty uncomfortable to travel during rush hour.

Paul: I suppose Tokyo is a very old city.

Keiko: It's not so old, but it's older than Sydney. It was built in the 15th century.

Paul: I thought it has always been the capital city.

Keiko: Well it became the capital in the 19th century; before that Kyoto was the capital of Japan.

Paul: Isn't Tokyo a coastal city like Sydney?

Keiko: Yes, it's on Honshu Island, on the north-east coast in Tokyo bay.

Paul: So is it as hot as Sydney? Do people go outdoors as much?

Keiko: No, we don't really have an outdoor lifestyle. For one thing it can be very hot in summer, but that's not a problem. Tokyo can be very humid.

Paul: It gets very humid here too. I bet it's not a very laid-back lifestyle.

Keiko: No, Tokyo is a very lively and dynamic city. People are always running to get somewhere.

Paul: How many universities are there in Tokyo?

Keiko: I think there are at least 13. There's always lots to do there.

Paul: Don't you find Sydney a bit boring?

Keiko: It's certainly quieter than home, but it's not boring at all. In fact, in many ways it's more attractive than Tokyo and I appreciate the fact that it isn't as busy or as noisy.

Paul: You can get some thinking space.

Keiko: And with the amount of work I've got, I need all the thinking space I can get.

CD 1 Track 42

So whereabouts are you from?

I suppose Tokyo is a very old city.

I thought it was always the capital city.

Isn't Tokyo a coastal city …

CD 2 Track 1

This city is partly in the south-east of Europe and partly in the west of Asia. It is a unique city in that it crosses two continents: Europe and Asia. It's a coastal city with the Bosphorous on one side and the Black Sea on the other. Although it has the largest population of that country, it isn't the capital city. It's an ancient city, founded by the Greeks and developed by the Romans and was the centre of two great empires. Nowadays it is a centre of finance and industry and is a very dynamic place. It's a beautiful city full of Islamic and Roman architecture, surrounded by impressive walls. In my opinion it is one of the most beautiful and interesting cities in the world.

CD 2 Track 2

Europe and Asia

the Bosphorous on one side and the Black Sea on the other

founded by the Greeks and developed by the Romans

CD 2 Track 3

Catherine: So Tao, how long are you staying in London for?

Tao: About three days.

Catherine: Lucky you. What are you going to do there?

Tao: Well I wanted to ask you that. I've got a map here; can you give me some suggestions?

Catherine: OK, I know London well. So, London has many districts, but at the heart of the city is Westminster; this is where Parliament and other government buildings are situated.

Tao: Oh, so Big Ben and the Houses of Parliament are there.

Catherine: Yes, but you can't see Big Ben. It's a huge bell in St Stephen's tower above the House of Commons.

Tao: But I can hear it.

Catherine: Oh yes; when you go to see the Houses of Parliament, you'll definitely hear it.

Tao: I'm definitely going there.

Catherine: Opposite Westminster on the other side of the river Thames is the South Bank. The South Bank is a

centre for the arts with galleries and theatres, but the most interesting thing there is the Globe Theatre.

Tao: Why is that interesting?

Catherine: It's Shakespeare's original theatre. They rebuilt it and now perform Shakespeare's plays there as they were performed in his time.

Tao: Well I'm not going there – I don't like Shakespeare.

Catherine: In that case you'll probably be more interested in the West End. There are modern theatres and clubs there; you could go to see a musical.

Tao: Now, that's better … I love musicals. I think I'll spend an evening in the West End.

Catherine: Near the West End is the City.

Tao: What does that mean? London is a city.

Catherine: It's the name of the financial and business district of London; it's where the Bank of England is and St Paul's Cathedral.

Tao: St Paul's Cathedral looks nice.

Catherine: It's really beautiful – you should go.

Tao: I will; I'd like to see that.

Catherine: What about museums? Are you interested in these?

Tao: Definitely, yes.

Catherine: There are lots and lots of them in London. The most famous one I suppose is in Bloomsbury. It's called the British Museum, but it's got lots of things from all over the world, including China.

Tao: Where's that again? I'd like to go there.

Catherine: It's in Bloomsbury, just north of Westminster. If you're still in London on Sunday morning you could go to Hyde Park near Bayswater. You can see people riding horses, you can go boating and you can hear people talking about different subjects at Speaker's Corner.

Tao: It sounds interesting, but we're coming back on Sunday morning so I don't think I'll have time to go there.

Catherine: Never mind. But you could still go to one of the markets on Saturday.

Tao: I love markets; they're so interesting.

Catherine: Go to Kensington Market then, in Kensington. Kensington is quite a well-off, wealthy part of London. You can buy almost anything there. There are about 1,000 stalls so you can spend ages looking around at things.

Tao: That sounds great. I love looking around at things in markets. I'll make time to go there.

Catherine. Well have a good time.

Tao : Thanks Catherine, I'm sure I will.

CD 2 Track 4

Lecturer: In today's lecture I'm going to look at the spread of cities into the countryside. I'll start with a brief look at the development of suburbs, then go on to their effect on human health and how we measure this.

Garden suburbs started in England, but it was in Australia that suburban living became the norm. During the 19th and 20th centuries, the Australian government encouraged suburban growth by funding services such as transport and education in local communities. Then railways were built to the new suburbs and by the 1890s as much as 40 per cent of Sydney's population lived in the suburbs. As in the USA, immigration helped – people who were not poor, but not rich enough to live in the city, bought homes in the suburbs.

In the USA suburban sprawl has become a headache for planners and politicians. Suburbs with low populations without good public transport means that everyone has to use cars and this is directly contributing to pollution. From 1990 the suburbs grew more rapidly than the cities in the US. These concerns have led to changes in planning strategy aimed at limiting the size of suburbs.

Development has very few restrictions in Southeast Asia. Two hundred years of city and suburban expansion in the West is being compressed into just 20 years of development. People prefer high-rise apartments, which means population densities are high, and the speed of development is breathtaking. One town near Seoul in Korea grew from nothing to half a million people in five years. Beyond the carefully built suburbs are the illegally built shanty towns populated by workers.

Despite the relative youth of Asian cities, traffic congestion has already become a problem because governments have not put in place public transport systems in the way the Australian government did 100 years ago. In the new cities there is no light rail system, so people have to use private transport and buses. Jakarta, for example, has become a very polluted city because of this.

Scientists try to measure suburban spread using the sprawl index (SI) – a calculation based on population density. The SI has been found to correlate with other facts. For example, in America a high sprawl index was shown to point to high obesity, or an overweight population, as people drove to the shops because they were too far away to walk. It also pointed to a high number of traffic deaths. Despite these problems, city building in Southeast Asia will continue at a fast pace as a product of economic development.

UNIT 8: Communication

CD 2 Track 5

Sara: What!

James: What is it? What's up, Sara?

Sara: Look at this bill for my mobile phone.

James: How much is it? Phew. That's a lot.

Sara: A lot? It's a small fortune. £164.50p. I don't believe it; that can't be right.

James: You must have used your phone a lot.

Sara: I don't use it very much at all, actually. I only call my mum, sister and a few close friends. No one else.

James : Well, let's have a look at the itemised bill.

Sara: What's that?

James: It shows the cost of each call and who you made the call to. How many minutes of free calls do you get each month?

Sara: 15 minutes, I think. And the line rental is about £30 a month.

James: That's good. Who do you rent your line from?

Sara: Turquoise.

James: OK. So let's check this bill. So, to 07776 281 443 you made four calls at off-peak time …

Sara: Yes, I try to call mum in the evening at least once a week.

James: And that didn't cost too much – £15.30. What's this one – 07887 683 702?

Sara: Say that again?

James: 07887 683 702. Who's that?

Sara: Never mind. Er, how much was it?

James: Not much.

Sara: So how come it's so expensive?

James: Here it is: 21st of August – 090 33 66 55, £50.

Sara: No way! £50? No way!

James: That's what it says here. Who did you phone?

Sara: Well, nobody.

James: I'm not sure I understand.

Sara: All right – two weeks ago someone rang and didn't leave a message. But it said 'missed call' on the phone and it had a number with it.

James: And you called that number back?

Sara: Maybe.

James: Maybe?

Sara: Yes, I didn't want to be rude.

James: And what happened when you called?

Sara: There was a very long answer phone message.

James: I see. Do you know how much you were charged for that call?

Sara: No, not really.

James: It was £20 a minute. You called for two and a half minutes, so that call cost you £50.

Sara: What?

James: Hang on. What's this? The same number again. Did you really call them twice?

Sara: Perhaps.

James: Another two and a half minutes?

Sara: Same message.

James: Another £50.

Sara: I don't believe it. I only called them again to tell them they had the wrong number.

James: I think they probably had the right number.

Sara: Surely there must be a mistake. They can't possibly charge anyone £20 a minute. It's against the law!

James: I'm afraid it's not. You called a premium rate line – you can usually tell by the first three numbers – and you did it twice. As soon as you call them, they charge you £20.

Sara: Well, this can't be right. I'm going to call the network operator to complain.

CD 2 Track 6

I don't believe it.
… that can't be right.
No way!
… there must be a mistake.

CD 2 Track 7

Sara: What's the number for the network?

James: If you look in the menu, the number is there.

Sara: My numbers. Yes, here it is.

Voice: Thank you for calling Turquoise. If you are calling about our latest adverts and want more information, press 1. If you would like to join Turquoise, press 2. For all other enquiries, please press 3. Please be advised that all calls may be recorded for training purposes.

Sara: Right – other enquiries.

Voice: Thank you. If you want more information about a recent order you have placed with Turquoise, please press 1. If you are an existing customer and you want to upgrade your phone, press 2. If you want to talk to someone, please press 3. Please press 4 if you want us to send you information about premium rate line call charges. If you want to join Turquoise from another network and bring your existing mobile number with you, please press 5. For all other enquiries, press 6. To hear these options again, press the hash key, or to return to the menu, press the star key.

Sara: Call charges – let me see what they say about this.

CD 2 Track 8

Sara: Hello, I'm calling about my recent mobile phone bill. I was overcharged for two calls I made.

Customer service advisor: Which calls do you mean exactly?

Sara: If you look at the two calls made on 5 May, you can see I was charged at a premium rate.

Customer service advisor: I'm afraid there's not much we can do if you called the number, unless you can show us that the call was made without your agreement.

Sara: No, but they didn't say how much the call cost.

Customer service advisor: When you ring a missed number, you must make sure who you're calling. As soon as you call, you're entering into an agreement with the company. Would you like us to bar that number in case they try it again?

Sara: Well, if there's nothing else you can do …

CD 2 Track 9

Isabelle: Oh yes … this is very handy – especially when I'm out of the house. It's quite small and it's very useful. It's made of aluminium, so it's very tough and light. If I need to remember something or if I have a good idea when I'm outside, instead of making notes I record myself and play it back when I get home. It's got a couple of buttons here for record and play and volume, and the battery goes into the back. The best thing about it is the length of time it can record for – about two hours – and that means I can take it to meetings, seminars and lectures. If I miss anything, I can play it back later.

Caroline: I carry this everywhere with me – I definitely couldn't live without it now. I've had it for about six months; I got it for my birthday last year. It's very light – light enough to strap onto my arm even though it's made of metal and plastic – and it's a lovely pink colour. It's only nine centimetres long, but it can hold up to 1,000 songs. I use it when I'm travelling or when I'm out running.

CD 2 Track 10

this is very handy
the best thing about it is
I carry this everywhere with me
I definitely couldn't live without it

CD 2 Track 11

Lecturer: Nowadays in the UK, two-thirds of the adult population have a mobile phone, with the average person spending £300 per year on call and rental charges. Of these people one-quarter considered their phone to be an essential part – not just an important part, but an essential part of their lives. So, as we can see, mobile phones in the last ten to 15 years have become an everyday item. But should we accept this situation without seriously thinking about the possible effects on our health? In today's lecture I'm going to look at the possible effects mobile telecommunications may have on humans, then move on to ways of taking precautions, or how to minimise the risks – if any – in using mobile phones. The main concerns about mobile phones centre around the transmitters, or antennae, used to send radio waves to and from the network.

We know that radio waves can heat up the skin and affect our nervous system; we have known this since the 1920s, in fact. People working with powerful radio waves complained of memory loss. They claimed they weren't able to remember things as well as they used to, and that they had loss of control over their movements and their heart rate. Following these observations, national guidelines were set for people working with powerful radio waves. Mobile phones are also, of course, small radios, but they use the lowest possible power. However, the government was concerned enough to set up an enquiry into mobile phone health concerns, which reported that there is no evidence of bad effects to our health caused by mobile phones but that gaps in our current medical knowledge mean that mobile phones cannot be called safe at the moment. In other words, we do not have enough knowledge of the effects of mobile …

CD 2 Track 12

… phones to say they are not dangerous, but from what we can see they do not have any significant harmful effects.

Let's look more closely at the issues. First, as we have seen, radio waves given out by mobile phones can heat up the skin. On the other hand, these radio waves do not seem to be powerful enough to cause damage to our bodies. Second, when people make long calls on their mobile phones, at the end they often complain of fatigue or tiredness, headaches and loss of concentration. However, under controlled conditions – in a laboratory, that is – the same results were not reported. The symptoms reported by the people could easily be due to other factors in modern-day living, such as stress. Third, it was found that mobile phone users are two and a half times more likely to develop cancer in parts of the brain next to the ear, but researchers say that there is no direct link or connection to mobile phone use. Finally, the International Agency for Research on Cancer found a relationship between childhood cancer and electrical power lines, which emit radiation – as do mobile phones. However, the radiation from power lines is a different kind of radiation with much more energy in contrast with the radiation coming from mobile phones. So it seems that any direct link with health problems is still unclear.

In order to find out more about these partially answered questions, physicists, neuroscientists and engineers are investigating three areas connected to mobile phone safety. These are, the effects of radio waves on blood pressure and our ability to concentrate, remember and learn. The second area is the link between mobile phone use and brain cancer and other forms of cancer. The third area of research is into the long-term effects of mobile phone use and looks into the health histories of people who have used mobiles from the 1980s. That's all I'd like to say about health issues, but given that there are concerns let's now turn to ways of minimising any possible risks to our health.

UNIT 9: Fitness and health

CD 2 Track 13

Lily: Paul! You've been playing that stupid game for hours! It's not healthy to spend all your time staring at a computer.

Paul: I've nearly completed level 5; I can't stop now. I'm really good at this game. Please, just let me finish this

then I'll do anything you like. Just give me another ten minutes. No, don't switch it off. Lily!

Lily: I'm sorry, Paul, but I'm starting to get worried about you. You look so pale and you're putting on weight, too. You spend all night playing that computer game, then immediately after classes you're playing it again. Look. It's a beautiful day outside; let's go and do something. Look at all the activities they have at the sports centre: rowing down on the lake, basketball at the sports hall, yoga in the Students' Union.

Paul: Well, maybe – but you know I'm no good at sports.

Lily: Oh, come on. You must play one sport.

Paul: I play a lot of sports and I'm useless at most of them.

Lily: Well there must be some sports you haven't had a go at.

Paul: I'm telling you – I've tried all of them and I'm hopeless at sport. I'm just not a natural sportsman.

Lily: You've tried every sport?! Are you being serious, or are you just trying to get out of it?

Paul: Alright – so maybe there are one or two sports I haven't had a try at.

Lily: What about windsurfing?

Paul: Uh … no thanks. I hate water and I hate being wet. I have no sense of balance and I'm not good at sailing. The last time I tried windsurfing was at school; when I finally managed to get on the thing the wind blew me to the other side of the lake and I had to walk three kilometres back with no shoes on.

Lily: OK. How about rugby?

Paul: Rugby?! Are you joking? You have to be big and strong and aggressive to play rugby.

Lily: Well, that depends on what position you play. What about this then? Kendo.

Paul: What's Kendo?

Lily: It says here that it's Japanese fencing – the way of the sword. You score points by hitting areas on your opponent's body.

Paul: Um … That sounds interesting.

Lily: You have to wear face masks and body armour.

Paul: I fancy having a try at that; I'm quite good with a sword. Do you fancy that?

Lily: Yes, I do actually. And there's a free beginner's course for students. There's a class this evening at 6 o'clock, and another one on Saturday morning at 10.15. Let's go and try it.

Paul: But don't we need all that special equipment? Swords, face protectors, armour and everything.

Lily: No, not at beginner level. It just says here, 'Wear loose clothing.' They can give us swords. It's at the Sturt gymnasium – we can catch a 286 bus there from the town centre. Come on. If we leave now, we can get there by 6.

Paul: OK, I'm coming.

CD 2 Track 14

I'm really good at this game.
I'm quite good with a sword.
… I'm no good at sports.
I'm useless at most of them.
… I'm not good at sailing.
… there must be some sports you haven't had a go at.
I fancy having a try at that …

CD 2 Track 15

Interviewer: Dr Rees, you attended Girton College at Cambridge during the 1940s, and won a full blue for swimming and a half blue for lacrosse. Can you explain what this means?

Dr Rees: Please, call me Joan. A blue is a person chosen to represent the university in sport. It began at Oxford and Cambridge, and any student who played in a match against the other university was awarded a blue. A full blue is given for senior sports such as athletics, cricket or rowing, and a half blue is given for minor sports. So lacrosse was seen as less important than swimming; therefore I only got a half blue for that.

Interviewer: I see. And what did you get when you became a blue?

Dr Rees: What you actually get is the right to wear a blue jacket, with a blue scarf or cap. But until 1948, women could not become members of the university even though they studied there, so in fact I never got my jacket. All the same, I am quite proud of my blues, along with my academic record.

Interviewer: Can you tell me more about lacrosse? It isn't often played these days.

Dr Rees: Yes, indeed. It's rather a violent game, in fact, originating in Canada with the Native Americans. It's played between two teams, with a sort of stick with a bag on the end, which is used to throw a very hard ball around. That's how I lost my tooth! I was the captain of the team, but there were only 12 women who played in those days, so we used to play against the men.

Interviewer: Do you still have any contact with the people you knew at Cambridge?

Dr Rees: Not really. I was invited to join The Tadpoles a few years ago, which is the old blues swimming club, but I have never been to the annual dinner.

Interviewer: What do you think of other universities awarding blues for sport?

Dr Rees: I think it's a very good idea.

Interviewer: Thank you, Joan.

CD 2 Track 16

Instructor: Right. First we'll do an easy one. This is the sitting position. Sit on the mat with your legs crossed and your hands on your knees. Keep your spine as straight as you can – that's very good, Lily – and your bottom flat against the floor. Breathe in and out nice and slowly and deeply, all the way in and out again, 5 – 10 times. Take your time. That's lovely. OK, now next time you breathe in, raise your arms up over your head. Right up, as far as you can stretch. Breathe out now, and bring your arms slowly down. I said slowly, Paul! Again - 5 – 7 times, until your arms are getting tired. Then stop. Now, here's one for all you animal lovers. It's called dog and cat. This is actually two positions, one following on from the other. We'll start with the dog. Get down on your hands and knees, keeping your hands just in front of your shoulders – that's it, you should feel balanced and comfortable in that position – just relax. Now spread your legs apart as wide as your hips. Breathe in, and at the same time, angle your hips up – no, that's not your hip Carmen that's better. Bend the spine down, dropping the stomach low, and raise your head up. Stretch those neck muscles. You're a dog, howling at the moon. OK, now we can move into the cat position. Raise the spine up again, that's it, you're a cat that's just seen a dog across the road, and angle the hips down. Pull your chest and stomach tight in again. Good. Start again. We're going to repeat this one several times. This will make your back stronger. Finally, here's one you probably did when you were at school - the half shoulder stand. First of all, lie on your back and lift your legs up into the air. Stretch them right up. Put your hands on your lower back to support the weight of your body, and put your elbows and your lower arms on the ground. You must take care that your weight is on your shoulders and upper back – not your neck. You could hurt yourself if the neck carries all the weight of the body. Breathe deeply in and out 5 – 10 times. That's it, lovely. When you want to come down come down, slowly lower your legs – slower than that, Paul. You must stay in control all the time. Keep your legs completely straight all the time. This will strengthen the muscles in your lower body. That's all for today. Well done. See you same time next week.

CD 2 Track 17

Stefan: Good afternoon and welcome to the fitness centre. My name is Stefan Ridley, you can find me in the Student's Union office during working hours. We're standing in the table tennis room at the moment, as you can see. If you would like to play, bats and balls are kept in this cupboard. Just ask anyone in the SU office. You don't have to be a member to use this facility – it's open to all students. We also have a full-size snooker table in this room to your left.

Student 1: Is this open in the evenings?

Stefan: Yes, it's open 24 hours a day, seven days a week. It costs £10 for six months, and if you pay this to me, I will give you a membership card. After that, you can use your card to get in, any time you like. You should join as soon as possible, as we have limited membership and it's very popular. We can't allow more than thirty members at one time, because it gets too busy.

Student 1: I'll pay you now.

Stefan: Let me show you round the gym first. That's over here, to your right.

Student 2: Yes, that's what I want to see. What equipment do you have? Do you have stair climbers?

Stefan: Yes, we have three. Come in and I'll show you. We'll start with the equipment to the left of the door, then clockwise round the room. The stair climbers are all in the cardio-vascular section, here near the door. You can walk, jog or run on the treadmill, the nearest to the door, the other two machines between them are for cycling, one lying down, the other sitting up. You can adjust the weight to make yourself work harder. You should use the cardio-vascular section to condition the heart, lungs and blood flow. But remember you shouldn't put too much weight on the machine – you could hurt yourself.

Student 3: I see you have a video machine there, in the corner next to the rowing machine. Are we allowed to bring our own videos?

Stefan: Yes, you can. There is also a CD player, so you can play your own music while you work out.

Student 3: Great. How much does it cost to join?

Stefan: It's £40 a year for students. It's open every day, all day and night, so you're allowed to come here at any time. I'm here during the day if you need any help or advice. Now, let's move on to the resistance equipment, which is along the wall to your right. These machines use weights to build up your muscles. First we have the leg curl bench. You have to lie down on your back, like this, then use your legs to lift the weights. This will strengthen your thighs and calf muscles. On the right of that is the cable cross machine, which has adjustable arms and is multi-use. You can adjust it to exercise any part of the body. You shouldn't try to use this on your own. Ask me for help to adjust the machine properly.

Student 2: Is there anything else we're not allowed to use alone?

Stefan: No, but the first time you use the gym you should do it during the day while I'm here. After that you can use it by yourself. Right. The next piece of equipment along this wall is the abdominal curl bench, where you can practise sit-ups and exercise the stomach muscles. To the right of that is the pec deck, which is very popular. Here you squeeze your elbows together – like this – to build up your chest. And this is the chin-up bar, against the other wall to your right again. Just take hold of the bar, like this, and raise up your whole body until your chin is level with the bar. Very good for strengthening the upper arms. Right, that's all from me, Are there any questions?

Student 3: Yes. Can we bring drink and food into the gym?

Stefan: You may bring a bottle of water or non-alcoholic drink in, but you may not bring in food of any kind.

Student 2: Are there any showers here?

Stefan: Yes, next door there are male and female showers, and there are also lockers for your valuables. You will have to supply your own lock for the lockers. Any more questions?

Student 1: Can I pay to join the snooker club now?

Stefan: Yes, of course. Come into my office. Does anyone else want to join the gym or the snooker club now?

Student 3: Yes, can I use my credit card?

CD 2 Track 18

You should join as soon as possible …

… the first time you use the gym you should do it during the day while I'm here.

… remember you shouldn't put too much weight on the machine …

You shouldn't try to use this on your own.

CD 2 Track 19

This piece of equipment is used to attach your board to your leg, so after falling off – again! – you don't have to go swimming back to the beach to get your board. It's an invaluable piece of equipment. It's attached to a thing near to the tail of your surfboard at one end and around the bottom of your back leg just above the ankle at the other. It's usually about ten foot long, made of nylon.

This is a kind of leg protection. They are made of very hard plastic and you wear them on the lower part of your leg, but only on the front. When you're playing, it means that if someone kicks you, it doesn't hurt so much.

There are a variety of these, depending on the different player positions. They are made of bars and are positioned across the front of the helmet. Basically, the more protection you have, the less you can see. Quarterbacks have the least protection as they need to see who they are passing the ball to, but linemen usually choose the greatest protection as they are more often involved in helmet-to-helmet combat.

These are really just three straight pieces of wood that the bowler tries to hit with a ball and a batsman tries to stop the ball hitting them. If the bowler hits these, the batsman is given out.

UNIT 10: RAG week

CD 2 Track 20

Sara: So what do you fancy doing during RAG week?

James: I haven't made up my mind yet, but I do want to do something.

Sara: Let's have a look at the list of things: it's divided into raids - or collections - and sponsored events.

James: I like the sound of raids – how about one of those?

Sara: The first one is on Saturday during the RAG parade in the centre of town.

James: Oh yes?

Sara: All students and staff are invited to join in – all student societies are expected to send at least two people. Who is going from the Film society?

James: I think Belen and Shin are going.

Sara: Didn't you fancy it?

James: Well I wasn't really sure what it was, so I kept quiet when they asked for volunteers.

Sara: Maybe it was for the best; for this year's parade everyone has to dress as a Viking.

James: A what?

Sara: A Viking – an ancient warrior from Scandinavia.

James: Imagine Shin dressed like a warrior. Do you think he knows about this?

Sara: Probably not.

James: So when's the next raid?

Sara: The next one is on Wednesday. Everyone is going to the coast to collect money there.

James: To the seaside, in February? I bet that's going to be cold. Any dressing up?

Sara: Er, no; dressing down. They're going in swimwear – trunks and bikinis.

James: Collecting in a bikini in February. Well, I don't think that's for me either.

Sara: How about a sponsored event?

James: How does that work? Any dressing up or down?

Sara: No, just going up or down.

James: Now what do you mean by that?

Sara: Well there's abseiling on Sunday.

James: What does abseiling involve?

Sara: It's just climbing down the side of a building with a rope.

James: Like climbing down a house?

Sara: No, like climbing down a 15-storey office block.

James: A 15-floor office block? No thanks. Isn't there anything I could do?

Sara: How about this … a sponsored hitch on Tuesday. You ask people to promise to give you money for the number of hours it takes you to get to a place – say 10 pence for every hour. Then, when you get back you collect the money and give it to the RAG rep.

James: What is the destination?

Sara: It's Dublin.

James: So what's the catch?

Sara: You have to get there with no money in the shortest possible time.

James: How am I supposed to get there with no money?

Sara: It's simple; you use your thumb.

James: Ah, you try to get drivers to stop and give you a lift. That sounds like something I could do – and I've always wanted to go to Dublin.

Sara: There's just one thing … You have to go with a partner.

James: Uh huh. What are you doing on Tuesday?

CD 2 Track 21

What's the catch?
What does abseiling involve?
What do you mean by that?
When's the next raid?
How does that work?

CD 2 Track 22

Speaker A: Oxfam is a charity which helps people in the developing world. When there is a crisis such as a war or natural disaster, they try to give food and water to people.

CD 2 Track 23

Speaker B: The organisation I'd like to talk about is a charity which helps people who have nowhere to live. It's called the Big Issue Foundation. Let me explain what it does. The organisation supplies homeless people with a magazine to sell. The people who sell it get, I think, 40 to 50 per cent of the cost of the magazine, so it gives them some money to live on. For example, in the centre of town here there's a Big Issue seller who I buy a copy from every month. I think it's interesting because, instead of just giving money to people, it helps them to work and gives them some respect. Furthermore, it's growing into an international organisation.

CD 2 Track 24

Speaker C: My favourite charity is the National Trust because I like walking and the countryside. I go walking every week and my favourite places to walk are all National Trust areas. And I don't have to pay to go there, so that's why I like the National Trust.

CD 2 Track 25

The organisation I'd like to talk about
Let me explain …
So it gives them some money
… who I buy a copy from

CD 2 Track 26

Vicky Chambers: Hello, thanks for coming. I'd like to introduce myself to everyone: my name is Vicky Chambers and I'm the student officer for Contact.

Contact's main activity is to put students from the university in contact with volunteer organisations in the city so that they can make a real contribution to the society around them. We try to develop links with local community groups and make the student experience at university a lot richer. So, let me tell you a bit more about what we do … the kinds of projects we run, the training we give to our volunteers, and the benefits students – especially international students – can get from joining a project.

We have a wide range of projects in many different areas so that students can bring the knowledge and skills they are learning in their course to practical use. We have projects in education where students can become a volunteer tutor in a state school and help children learn how to read for example. If you are studying information technology, you could work on an IT project. Many organisations around the city need people with good computing skills to teach other people how to use a computer and to set up databases and accounting programmes. Have you got retail, research, marketing or management skills? There are many charity shops in the area who need assistants in sales, marketing and fundraising. You could help with the latest campaign, you may be asked to do market research for a charity or you might simply work in the shop and sell things to customers. Or are you good at languages? We have many projects which need translating and interpreting skills, from people who are new in the community, to working with the legal or law system for example.

Although you do not need any previous volunteering experience to get involved in Contact, we do ask you to go for a training day with us. We're not simply going to throw you in at the deep end; we're here as part of a full support service to make your volunteer experience enjoyable and useful. The training day helps to prepare you for working with charities. As part of the training day there is a morning induction session. There are three aims of the induction session: first, to help you to match your skills, abilities and interests to the projects available; second, to explore the characteristics of a successful volunteer – that is, what makes a good volunteer; and third, to meet the other staff and students who are volunteering. You may well have further in-house training from the charity in addition to this.

So, why volunteer? Why come to Contact? Well, volunteering is an excellent opportunity to gain experience and develop skills in your subject area. When you get involved in a project you are able to put your knowledge into practice. It can help your confidence and help your personal and professional development. Employers like to see that students have experience in volunteering; it means they have gained skills and experience that otherwise they do not have – and this makes you a better choice for the job you want. For international students you get the opportunity to meet people, to practise and improve your English and, very importantly, you have the chance to explore and understand the culture you are living in. Finally, perhaps the best thing about volunteering is the satisfaction you get from helping other people.

CD 2 Track 27

Lecturer: In the first term we looked at how the state, or government agencies, work in society through organisations like hospitals in the health service, schools in the education service and other organisations in the welfare system – that is, the system by which the government tries to help the people in society who, for whatever reason, need help – to give people a better standard of living. Then, in the last lecture, I looked at how charities work alongside state agencies and in some cases, instead of government agencies, to help people in society. Now I'm going to compare people's attitudes to welfare in two welfare systems – that is, in Europe and America. Why and in what ways are America and Europe so far apart in social policy? Alesina and Glaeser examined three beliefs about poverty in the different societies and found significant differences between the two.

The first belief is that the poor are trapped in poverty. They reported that in Europe 60 per cent of people hold this belief, but only 29 per cent of Americans believe this. The second is that luck determines income. Again there is a big difference here – 54 per cent of Europeans held this belief, whereas 30 per cent of Americans believed this. Finally is the belief that the poor are lazy. In contrast with the previous statements, 60 per cent of Americans believed this whereas only 24 per cent of Europeans thought this.

Alesina and Glaeser go on to describe how income is shared differently by the welfare systems and the reasons for this difference. Looking at how much money the governments spend on welfare we can see that in America 30 per cent of gross domestic product goes on welfare. In comparison, it is 45 per cent – including healthcare spending – in Europe. Of this 45 per cent, two-thirds is on welfare. Americans, by contrast, are more likely to give money privately. In 2000 Americans gave almost US$700 per person to charity compared with US$141 in Britain and just US$57 in Europe.

They put forward interesting explanations for the causes of this difference including politics and geography. First, politics: they point out that American political structures are older than political structures in Europe and are more conservative. Political structures in America were set up almost 200 years ago. Europe, however, has seen many changes in the past century with many European countries having proportional representation in their political system. This has meant that socialist parties have been represented better. They point out that there is a relationship between the age of the political structure and its friendliness towards the welfare system.

Next, geography. In Europe, geography increased the power of the labour movement. The geography of the United States, however, limited the power of the labour movement. Let's take an example. In a small country like Belgium, labour unrest could have a big national impact, whereas labour unrest in a large country like America had less impact. The next thing was the effect of war. In the 20th century, Europe saw a century of war, but the geography of America and its economic strength protected it from war. Countries that saw war on their territory were more likely to set up new institutions which gave more power to the left. The next point they look at is racial diversity …

UNIT 11: Work

CD 2 Track 28

Paul: Lily, you've got to help me with this … I need money.

Lily: Well, I haven't got any.

Paul: I mean, I'm going to apply for a job and I want you to help me choose.

Lily: Are you finding it hard to live on your grant?

Paul: It's impossible to live on a student grant. I've already spent it on university fees and accommodation.

Lily: Really? So going out every night isn't anything to do with being hard up?

Paul: Maybe a bit, but I try to keep my spending down as much as I can. I try to save as much as possible, but I'm completely broke.

Lily: Let's have a look at the 'Jobs' section at the back of the paper. Here we are: 'Positions vacant'. What about this one? 'Kitchen hand required for busy restaurant. Must be reliable with some experience.'

Paul: Aah … What's the pay like?

Lily: It doesn't really say, just that it's 'above average'.

Paul: What are the hours like?

Lily: Well, it's part-time in the mornings.

Paul: I'd rather not work in the morning; I've got quite a few lectures then and I wouldn't like to miss any.

Lily: How about this one then? 'Shop assistant required in bakery for day and night work. Must be a team player.'

Paul: A 'team player'. Well that sounds like me, but I wouldn't want to work at night – I've got a busy social life to keep up.

Lily: So when are you prepared to work?

Paul: I wouldn't mind working at the weekend, perhaps.

Lily: I'll have a look. Here's one … 'Care worker required on a casual basis. Friendly, considerate person needed for Saturday morning work.'

Paul: Morning again. I'd prefer to work in the afternoon. I don't like getting up early at the weekend. But I like the idea of being a part-time care worker – helping other people – and it will be good when I apply for a full-time job.

Lily: That's all there is in the part-time section I'm afraid.

Paul: What's the rate of pay?

Lily: It's OK: $12 per hour; four hours each week.

Paul: I don't know if I could do it or not. I'm quite friendly, but am I considerate? What do you think, Lily?

Lily: Well you do try to think about other people and help them when you can … so, yes, I think you could say you're considerate.

Paul: Let me have the phone number, then. I'll give them a call to see if the job's still going.

Lily: It's 040 931 602.

Paul: Sorry, what was that again?

Lily: 040 931 602 … and good luck – I hope you get something.

CD 2 Track 29

I'd rather not work in the morning …
I wouldn't want to work at night …
I wouldn't mind working at the weekend …
I'd prefer to work in the afternoon.

CD 2 Track 30

Andrew: Hello, you must be Paul, come in and take a seat.

Paul: Thanks very much.

Andrew: Let me introduce ourselves, I'm Andrew Clark and I'm the director of the Canberra Care Agency, and this is our Personnel Officer Arzu.

Arzu: Nice to meet you.

Paul: Good to meet you too.

Andrew: I'll tell you a little bit about the agency and the job and then we'd like to ask you a few questions. After that you can ask us any questions you might have – does that sound OK?

Paul: Yes, that's perfectly fine.

Andrew: Arzu – would you like to tell Paul about us?

Arzu: Yes, we are a local government agency established about ten years ago with the aim of providing extra help to older people in the community, particularly at times of the year when their full-time carer is away or is on a break. We started as a small-scale voluntary agency, expanded, became part of local government and we are continuing to expand year on year.

Paul: And this position is to cover for someone on a Saturday mornings?

Arzu: That's right – Saturday mornings at the moment, but it might increase to more days – would you be interested in more hours?

Paul: Yes, definitely, although Saturday morning is fine for the moment.

Arzu: Good. Our workers do things like do the shopping, cleaning and gardening and of course socialising which is an important part of the job.

Paul: That's fine – I enjoy chatting.

Arzu: Now Andrew will ask you a few questions about yourself, if that's okay?

Paul: Yes, perfectly fine.

Andrew: Now, on your application form it says at present you are a student studying at the University of Canberra and you are in your first year, is that right?

Paul: Yes, that's right – I started my course this year.

Andrew: And what are your interests?

Paul: I like reading, surfing and music. In fact, I'm a member of the student radio station – I have my own radio programme on Wednesday night.

Andrew: That's interesting. Do you think any of your interests might help you in this job?

Paul: Certainly, people always like talking about books and music.

Andrew: And what other personal qualities do you think you could bring to the job?

Paul: I'm hard-working and practical so any small jobs that need doing around the house or garden I can do quite easily.

Andrew: And finally, if we were to offer you the job, when would you be available to take it?

Paul: When would I be available to take up the job? I don't see why I wouldn't be able to start immediately.

Andrew: Now, is there anything you would like to ask us?

Paul: Just one question, if you don't mind.

Andrew: Please go ahead.

Paul: Are the people who need help in the Hawker district or around Canberra.

Andrew: Well, in fact they are all over the region, but we try our best to give care workers a person who lives as close as possible to them. Now according to your application form you live in University accommodation.

Paul: That's right – I'm in the University village.

Andrew: There should be no problem finding someone for you then – in fact the person we have in mind lives quite close by.

Paul: I see, thanks.

Andrew: Well thank you very much for coming. It was very nice to meet you.

Arzu: Yes, thanks for coming. Have a good journey back.

Andrew: Yes, thanks for waiting. Have a great journey back.

CD 2 Track 31

Well thank you very much for coming.

It was very nice to meet you.

Yes, thanks for coming. Have a good journey back.

Good to meet you, too. Hope to see you again soon.

CD 2 Track 32

Receptionist: Hello … Welcome to the Careers Advice Service. What can we do for you?

Student: I'm not sure really. I'm a first year student, and I'd like to know what the Careers Advice Service does and the resources that are available to students.

Receptionist: OK, well I can let you know about most of what we have here and what we do. First of all you're here at the information desk. From here you can book an interview with a careers adviser, reserve prospectuses and information booklets, get a place on one of our workshops, and book places to go to recruitment fairs and visit employers.

Student: I see; so this is the starting point?

Receptionist: Only if you want to do those specific things or if you need more help to find what you want. Most students' starting point is over there in the reading room.

Student: That's the area with desks and chairs?

Receptionist: That's correct. We hold a lot of information on other university courses – mainly postgraduate – and on employers, plus information on businesses, companies and other organisations.

Student: Such as?

Receptionist: Such as the Civil Service and other public services. So we hold all the general information there, but just behind that is our dedicated careers information room with up-to-date information on occupations, vocational training, travel abroad and prospective employers.

Student: And that's just over there, behind those chairs?

Receptionist: That's right. In the room next to me, just there, you can see a computer cluster room.

Student: Uh huh.

Receptionist: We use the cluster room for two main things. First, we have our online vacancy system, which provides information on thousands of jobs with hundreds of employers. It includes details of graduate jobs, full-time and part-time jobs, and is updated almost daily. The second thing we have in there is a program that gives information on all aspects of career planning. The program identifies your needs by asking you relevant questions and then gives you advice according to your answers.

Student: Well, that's amazing. Does it really work?

Receptionist: Of course it does, and we're continually developing it. Behind the careers information room is our seminar room. This is where we hold workshops.

Student: What kinds of subjects do you cover?

Receptionist: We have workshops on job-hunting techniques, how to write a curriculum vitae, how to do well at interviews – interview techniques – and how to deal with employer selection tests.

Student: Employer selection tests? You mean that even after exams the employer gives us more tests?

Receptionist: Yes, I'm afraid that nowadays more and more employers do that. And then finally, along the back wall are the career advisors' offices. We always try to have one of the specialist advisors available during the Service's office hours. They are there to give you advice on your careers and prospects, to give training and workshops.

Student: But students only see them in their final year.

Receptionist: Oh no. No, it's a really good idea to make an appointment with them in your first year, or as soon as you know what you want to do after graduation. They can give you guidance about things to do alongside your course, which will help you to get a job later.

Student: So I should really book an interview now?

Receptionist: Yes, it is in your interests to do so.

Student: I'd also like to go to one of those workshops too – the one about employer's tests.

Receptionist: We'll fix you up with that right now. Are you free on Wednesday afternoon at 1?

Student: I think so.

Receptionist: Then we'll arrange for you to see Ms Hussein, and the next workshop is next month – March 2nd at 10 am in the seminar room.

Student: That's Ms Hussein on Wednesday at 1 and the workshop on March 2nd at 10.

Receptionist: That's right.

Student: Well thank you very much; you've been really helpful.

CD 2 Track 33

Maryam: This is the third workshop from the Careers Advice Service in our series of workshops about job-hunting. My name is Maryam Hussein, and if you have any questions please stop me and ask. Today I'll be looking at types of tests used by employers in the recruitment and selection process. These types of test are usually known as psychometric tests – and put more simply this means measurement of the mind. Such tests have been around a long time – they were devised at the beginning of the 20th century as part of research into social science, and then in the 1970s they were adapted for recruitment purposes. Today these tests are seen as a key item in the recruitment process as they offer an alternative way of assessing candidates to qualifications and traditional interviews.

There are really two kinds of psychometric test: aptitude and personality tests. The aptitude test is basically an IQ test, and aims to test your ability at work or study. Aptitude tests are not tests of general knowledge. Many aptitude tests are designed to measure a particular ability, for example verbal, numerical, diagrammatic, abstract reasoning or data interpretation. In general, aptitude tests usually consist of verbal, numerical and diagrammatic sections done with multiple-choice questions. Verbal tests are usually in the form of a passage, followed by a number of statements. The candidate must decide if the statements are true, false or if you cannot tell from the information. Numerical tests assess your mathematical ability, diagrammatic tests find out how good you are at working with diagrams, abstract reasoning tests your ability to think logically and data interpretation tests your ability to use data to make a decision. The tests are often done under exam conditions and are timed, a typical test might allow 30 minutes for thirty questions. Your score is compared with other people's scores on the test. The other people are called the norm group and could be other students, a more general group or people already in the job. This helps the people selecting candidates for the job to compare your reasoning skills with others. In general, the earlier the test is used in the selection process, the more important it is. If the aptitude test is used before the interview, there will be a pass mark, so if you passed the test you are to go forward to the interview. If the test is used later, it is just one part of the selection. Other parts could include group activities, presentations and so on.

In order to prepare for an aptitude test, you could ask the employer for some example questions, do practice tests, and practise with word games, mathematical games and puzzles with diagrams. You can also find examples of these tests on the Internet. We have books and leaflets on these tests in the reading section of the Careers Advice Service. If it is a long time since you did any maths, practise by doing some basic activities.

The second kind of test is the personality test. The aim of these tests is to find out about your personality from your reactions to a number of questions or statements. This type of test is more like a questionnaire and focuses on things like how well you work in a team, how honest you are, what motivates you and your attitude to life. There are no right or wrong answers to these questions and usually there is no time limit. It is best to try to answer the questions as honestly as possible. The purpose of this kind of test is to make sure that the successful candidate fits well into the culture of the company and will enjoy working in that environment.

Now let me give you an example of an aptitude test question which assesses verbal reasoning. …

CD 2 Track 34

A: Looking for a new job? What's wrong with your job now? I thought you liked it.

B: It's okay, but I don't feel it's enough somehow. I don't really get job satisfaction.

A: Why do you need job satisfaction? You earn lots of money: your monthly salary is more than I get in a year.

B: Actually, I think there are more important things in a job than just how much you earn.

A: Such as?

B: Such as the number of hours for example. Yes, I do get a good salary, but look at the number of hours I work: 24/7 – I even dream about work.

A: Well do you want to know what I think? In my view, the most important thing is job security. It's important to know that your job is safe.

B: I don't know really. I always think about becoming a teacher – they get great holidays, and time for yourself is really important.

A: A teacher gets great holidays! You're joking, the only holidays a teacher gets are working holidays: marking homework, school trips, setting exams. A teacher gets great holidays – really.

B: Well, all right. Maybe not a teacher, but I just think my work environment – the place I work could be better. I'm in an office most of the time, I would be great to work outdoors.

A: Like a farmer?

B: Not especially, but out of an office, working with your hands – real work, not sat at a computer all day. What do you think?

A: Personally, I think that you have a great job. You work in a team, and that's important. People in traditional jobs often work alone a lot of the time and it's hard work too.

B: That's true, but think of the amount of responsibility I have – there's a lot of pressure on me.

A: Oh, come on. The amount of responsibility you have? What about someone like a surgeon – now that's real responsibility.

B: I suppose you're right.

A: And think about the respect you get for the responsibility you have.

B: That's true too.

A: And you get a good salary because of the amount of responsibility.

B: Okay, I've changed my mind – maybe it's not so bad after all.

UNIT 12: Academic success

CD 2 Track 35

Tutor: And after James gives his presentation, Carmen, it's over to you. Can you give us a short outline of your topic? What was your research about? Memory and learning, wasn't it?

Carmen: Yes, I'm going to give a brief review of how we remember things.

Tutor: Sorry, Carmen. Come in.

Paul: I'm so sorry I'm late.

Tutor: We're just going over the list of presentations today. Carmen is just outlining the subject of her presentation. Can I remind you that you should be punctual to tutorials?

Paul: I'm really sorry, I didn't remember to set the alarm last night and …

Tutor: Yes, I think you can spare us the details. Carmen, I apologise for interrupting you; please continue.

Carmen: OK – so I did my project on how memory works and …

Tutor: Hold on a minute Carmen. What's the trouble, Paul?

Paul: I … er … I haven't got a pen.

Tutor: You haven't got a pen?

Paul: I'm afraid not. I think I left it on the bus.

Tutor: Could anyone lend Paul a pen, please?

Carmen: Here you are.

Paul: Thanks Carmen. I'm very sorry.

Carmen: So, where was I?

Tutor: You were talking about how memory works.

Carmen: Yes, that's right and I'll also go on to talk about the way in which people store and retrieve information in their long-term memories.

Tutor: Well that sounds very interesting. So that's James followed by Carmen. Then next on the list is, ah – it's you, Paul.

Paul: Me?

Tutor: Yes – that's what we agreed last month.

Paul: Oh no! It completely slipped my mind. I'm really sorry – I haven't finished it yet. I absolutely forgot it's for today. I was convinced it's for next week.

Tutor: No, it was for today – as we agreed a month ago.

Paul: Will it be all right if I do it for next week?

Tutor: Are you able to give us a summary of the main points?

Paul: I really can't remember them, I'm afraid.

Tutor: So you forgot to do your presentation for today and you can't remember the main points either. Well, I'm afraid we're going to have a shorter tutorial than usual today. On the positive side, we'll be able to give James and Carmen our full attention and have more time for discussion and questions. So James, over to you …

CD 2 Track 36

I'm so sorry I'm late.
I apologise for interrupting you …
I'm very sorry.
It completely slipped my mind.
I absolutely forgot it's for today.
I was convinced it's for next week.
I really can't remember them, I'm afraid.

CD 2 Track 37

Paul: What am I going to do, Lily? James is angry with me because we need a double tutorial next week, the Professor doesn't believe that I've done any work and Carmen is furious because she had 15 minutes of questioning about her presentation instead of five.

Lily: You've got to get organised, Paul. If you can't remember anything and forget what you need to do for each term, you need a plan.

Paul: Oo … OK, where do I start?

Lily: Make a list of things you have to do for university each week – things like lectures, tutorials and seminars … things that are fixed at regular intervals.

Paul: So, like going to the gym.

Lily: Paul we're talking about work here, not your personal life.

Paul: Sorry.

Lily: Then you need to think about how much work you have to do for each of these.

Paul: Like preparation.

Lily: That's right; go over the reading list for each course and the list of lectures and try to plan well in advance what you need to do and how much of it there is.

Paul: Basically a study timetable.

Lily: That's correct – a timetable. Then finally you need to put in the other work we have to do like long essays and exams; you really can't forget an exam or turn up late to one of those.

Paul: So, put in all the long-term work, so that I'll be ready for it.

Lily: That's right.

Paul: I'm really not looking forward to the exams.

Lily: So are you feeling a bit nervous about the test tomorrow?

Paul: There's a test tomorrow? What is it? Why didn't anyone tell me?

Lily: Paul, you're hopeless!

CD 2 Track 38

Lecturer: Today I'm going to talk about how our memory works and the three stages of memorising something. We rely on our memories to help us through each day. The pieces of information that we use are stored in our memories like information in a filing cabinet. But the information needs to be well organised so that it can be easily retrieved for later use.

Scientists today think that the memory goes through three stages: immediate memory, short-term memory and long-term memory. Some people also refer to the three Rs of memory: registration, retention and retrieval.

Let's look at the first of the three R's – registration. Our senses register and compare information in our immediate memory. Our immediate memory is therefore also known as sensory memory because it holds information coming in from the senses for very brief periods, less than a second. This information is either rejected or passed on to the short-term memory storage.

The short-term memory can hold about seven items at one time. Information it holds is easily disturbed and if it is not rehearsed immediately it will be forgotten within about 30 seconds. Short-term memory is used when we want to hold information temporarily – for example, a telephone number or figures in mental arithmetic. While something is in short-term memory parts of it are being selected to go into long-term memory and the rest is being rejected – that is, forgotten. Our short-term memory is, in effect, the in-tray of the brain.

If the short-term memory is the in-tray of the brain, then our long-term memory, in contrast, is the filing cabinet – and I'd like to have a look at this now. Our long-term memory can store any number of pieces of information and can last for a lifetime. Some psychologists divide long-term memory into two kinds: episodic and semantic. Episodic memory consists of remembering incidents such as childhood recollections or a film you saw. In effect it is the story-telling part of the memory. Semantic memory consists of remembering knowledge about the world – for example, the name of a mountain or city or the meaning of words. It is our combined dictionary and encyclopaedia.

So how do we call-up these memories? Let's look now at retrieval – how we actually bring back information we have remembered. Well, sounds, smells, tastes, sights, places and moods can all conjure up memories of past events. Most people, however, remember better things they have heard or seen. If you have a good auditory memory you will be able to remember things you hear such as a tune or language better than things you see. You will learn better by listening or reading out loud. A good visual memory means that you are best at remembering things you see, such as the layout of a room or the details of a picture. You will learn better by reading – that is, seeing words

CD 2 Track 39

Lecturer: So hello everyone and welcome to the second in our series of workshops about improving the way we study. In the first session last week we looked at preparing a study timetable, especially leading into the exam period. In this session we're going to look at good study techniques, so if there are any questions, please feel free to stop me and I'll try to answer them.

I've divided the workshop into three basic sections: the first is how our bodies affect our memory; the second is how our emotions affect our ability to remember; the final section is how revision can help us. Let's begin with the physical part of remembering. Research has shown that stress reduces our ability to learn – so before you sit down to study, some simple relaxation activities can help.

Student 1: Do you mean running or swimming or something?

Lecturer: Well, it is important to be in good physical shape, but I mean something much more simple like taking ten deep breaths and relaxing your shoulders. Nothing that needs too much effort. The next thing is diet: drink plenty of water, eat a little and often, and be careful of what you eat. Food with lots of protein like fish, eggs and meat help the memory. Too many carbohydrates can slow your brain down.

Student 2: Which foods contain carbohydrates?

Lecturer: Things like sugar, bread and potatoes - try to avoid eating these or any other sweet food.

Student 1: But I can't live without chocolate – especially when I'm studying.

Lecturer: Well, maybe you could eat less of it. … The next thing is to take short breaks. We remember the first and last things in a list best, so by giving yourself short breaks you create opportunities for your brain to remember the first and last things. The final thing is sleep – don't stay awake all night worrying or revising. When we are awake we're picking up thousands of pieces of information, but when we sleep it appears the brain is storing this information and making sense of it. Perhaps this is why our dreams are often about what happened during the day. Sleep is an essential process of storing and filing information.

Student 1: So is staying in bed part of our education?

Lecturer: Ha! Yes, in a way – but not during lectures. Now, for the emotional part of studying.

Our emotions affect how well we learn. I mentioned earlier that stress makes learning difficult. In the same way, we learn better when we feel good. It also helps when we are interested in what we are learning. Similarly, in order to remember something you must pay attention and concentrate on it. Learning is very difficult if you are thinking about something, or someone, else.

The next thing to understand is what we are studying. If we can't understand something then it's very difficult to learn it. Ask someone to help you with a difficult subject; your tutor will always be happy to explain difficult ideas or topics.

Student 2: Yes, our department has regular drop-in sessions where students can ask about anything on the course so far.

Lecturer: And that's important. Knowing you can get help can improve your confidence, and confidence is a key point. People who think they can't study often don't study well because they tell themselves they are not good learners. Try to be positive about yourself and your learning; be confident and don't worry about making mistakes. If you're not making mistakes you're simply not learning.

Student 1: In that case, I've probably learnt more than anyone on my course.

Lecturer: Don't let mistakes worry you. Finally, revising. It is thought that as much as 70 per cent of what we learn in a day will be forgotten by the next day. Reviewing what you learnt has a great result on learning. Get into the habit of frequently revising things you have learnt. Just half an hour a week can have a great effect. And finally, you can learn things more quickly if you rehearse it to yourself aloud; it makes you use your ears as well as your eyes.

CD 2 Track 40

analysing
happening
using
seeing
having
planning

CD 2 Track 41

A: I'm getting more forgetful as I get older I'm afraid, but I still have quite a good memory, especially for faces – in other words once I meet a person I can usually remember their face and where I met them. As for remembering their name, I may or may not remember this, but their face – yes. As for dates, I'm hopeless at remembering dates and numbers. In fact, the last thing I forgot was my sister's birthday.

B: Have I got a good memory? Yes, I think so. I never forget a name, by that I mean once I've learnt the name of someone or something I'm pretty good at remembering it. It can take me a long time to learn it, though. I'm usually good at remembering people's faces too, and I never forget important dates. So names, faces and dates, I'm fine with. Now, what was the last thing I forgot? The last thing I forgot was five things on the shopping list. I don't like shopping and I often forget to buy things. I guess, what I mean to say is that I forget things I don't like doing.

C: I've got a terrible memory, I am so forgetful you wouldn't believe it. Can I remember names? Only the names of people who are close to me. Faces, not really. After a few days from meeting someone I don't usually recognise them, which can be a bit embarrassing. I'm a bit better with dates, I can usually remember birthdays and other important dates. The last things I forgot were my house keys. I left them at work and had to go back to the office to pick them up again.

CD 2 Track 42

What I mean to say is …
… by that …
In other words …
Let me put it another way …
To put it differently …

Marshall Cavendish ELT
119 Wardour Street
London W1F 0UW

Editorial, design and production by Hart McLeod, Cambridge

Printed and bound by

Acknowledgements

Text: p.8 A Guaranteed Good Time taken from A Fresher's Guide to Life, University and Everything by Ian Comerford; p.17 Universities in Britain taken from Universities ©Hobsobs, www.studyuk.hobsons.com; p.24 Charts 4 and 5, based upon www.immi.gov.au/study/overview/index.htm statistics, Chart 6, based upon www.ucas.com/figures/ucasdata/region/ continent.html; p.29 Based upon An equal share of housework makes a happy relationship; p.38 Welcome to the Media, Film and Cultural studies course ©Adrian Mackenzie, Lancaster University; p.39 Media studies: The next generation by Jonathon Duffy, thanks to BBC News and Jonathon Duffy, http://news.bbc.co.uk/go/pr/fr/-/2/hi/uk_news/magazines/3444499.stm; p.45 Selection of biggest grossing films to 2004, based upon All-Time Worldwide Boxoffice, http://imdb.com/boxoffice/ alltimegross?region=world-wide; p.48 Cue FM taken from What is Cue FM? Want to be a DJ?, thanks to University of Canberra Union, http://ucu.canberra.edu.au/tc/site.php?id=319; p.50 Question 2 based upon, A new planet or queen of comets?, Jeff Hecht, New Scientist, 20 March 2004; S Korea launches high speed train, thanks to BBC News, http://news.bbc.co.uk/1/hi/world/asia-pacific/3589591.stm; EMI jettisons 1,500 jobs and 200 acts, Dan Milmo ©The Guardian; p.52 Reuters: the business of news taken from Reuters Group PLC, http://encarta.msn.com/encyclopedia_ 761591320/ Reuters_Group_PLC.html; Early History, thanks to Reuters, http://about.reuters.com/aboutus/history; p.55 Question 3, based upon The Internet Changes the Way News Is Gathered, Poynteronline previously taken from The American Journalist in the 21st Century; p.60 Hydropower: the fascinating facts based upon, Hydropower, http://en.wikipedia.org/wiki/Hydropower, ©2000, 2001, 2002 Free Software Foundation, Inc. 59 Temple Place, Suite 330, Boston, MA 02111-1307 USA. Everyone is permitted to copy and distribute verbatim copies of this license document but changing it is not allowed; How Hydropower Plants Work, http://howstuffworks.com/index.htm; p.65 Biomass energy: a definition, based upon RENEWABLE ENERGY: Biomass Energy, http://www.yptenc.org.uk/docs/factsheets/env_facts/ biomass_energy.html; p.68 SUPER SUN POWER, based upon 25 ways to save the planet, http://www.cat.org.uk/information/howgreen.tmpl?cart=1081424617295398&subdir=information; p.72 Sydney, based upon http://brainencyclopedia.com/encyclopedia/s/sy/sydney.html; p.74-75 Megacities: a new kind of city based upon Modernization, Britannica; p.77 Questions 5 and 6, based upon High-rise sprawl, Geographical, May 2004; p.78 City populations 1950–2015, based upon Department of Economic and Social Affairs, United Nations Secretariat, World Urbanization Prospects; p.81 Avoiding phone scams, based upon New missed call phone scam, CBBC Newsround, http://news.bbc.co.uk/cbbcnews/hi/sci_tech/newsid_3499000/3499415.stm; Text scam warning for consumers, BBC News Online, http://news.bbc.co.uk/2/hi/technology/2446363.stm; p.82 Mobile communication: back to basics, based upon How Cell Phones Work, http://electronics.howstuffworks.com/cell-phone1.htm; Mobile phone, Wikipedia, http://en.wikipedia.org/ wiki/Mobile_phone ©2000, 2001, 2002 Free Software Foundation, Inc. 59 Temple Place, Suite 330, Boston, MA 02111-1307 USA. Everyone is permitted to copy and distribute verbatim copies of this license document but changing it is not allowed; p.85-6 The effect of mobile phones on human health, based upon Hot Topics-Mobile Phone Safety, thanks to BBC News, http://www.bbc.co.uk/print/science/

hottopics/mobilephones/print.shtml; p.94-5 Work out what's important ©The Independent, 21 June 2004; p.97 EVERY STEP COUNTS, based upon Stars join the fitness craze that makes every step count, The Observer, 22 August 2004; p.99 RAG, thanks to BBC News and Ellie Murch, http://www.bbc.co.uk/northyorkshire/students/rag/index.shtml; p.101 CHARITABLE TRUSTS taken from The eccentric world of British Philanthropy by Helen McGavin ©The Independent, 2 June 2004; p105 Question 6, Economics focus/Why welfare? ©The Economist Newspaper Limited, London, March 13th 2004; p.111 The Balanced Workers of Tomorrow, Liane Katz © Copyright Guardian Newspapers Limited 2003; p.115 based upon http://www.sussex.ac.uk/cdec/careerinfo/ci_psycho.html; p.125 Synaesthasia: mixing the senses, based upon Kaleidoscope Eyes: The Secrets Of A Novel Gift, thanks to the University of Melbourne and Science Daily.

Photos: p.2 ©Tom Stewart/Corbis; p.4 ©Lisa Woollett/Photofusion Picture Library/Alamy; p.7 A ©Camera Crew Photography and University of Bradford, B ©Charles Gupton/Corbis, C ©Zefa/Ausloeser; p.8 ©Chuck Savage/Corbis; p.10 ©Christa Stadtler/Photofusion Picture Library/Alamy; p.15 A ©Dominic Burke/Alamy, B ©Camera Crew Photography and University of Bradford, C ©Camera Crew Photography and University of Bradford; p.16 ©SOAS used by courtesy of SOAS, University of London; p.18 ©Trevor Smithers ARPS/Alamy; p.19 ©Jacky Chapman/Janine Wiedel Photolibrary/Alamy; p.20 ©David Butow/Corbis; p.21 ©2004 University of Victoria.Reproduced with permission; p.25 ©BananaStock/Alamy; p.26 Dynamic Graphics Group/Creatas/Alamy; p.32 A ©Robert Estall/Corbis, B ©Paul Thompson/Eye Ubiquitous/Corbis, C ©Benedict Luxmoore/Arcaid/ Alamy, D ©David Martyn Hughes/Alamy, bottom left ©Elizabeth A. Whiting/Elizabeth Whiting & Associates/Corbis, bottom right ©Zefa/ Masterfile/Albert Normandin; p.36 both ©Brian Hall used with kind permission, bottom left ©George McLeod; p.38 ©Michael Pole/Corbis; p.39 ©Franco Vogt/Corbis; p.41 ©David Butow/Corbis; p.42 A ©J. Wenk/ Columbia Pictures/Corbis, B ©David Appleby/Buena Vista Pictures/Corbis, C ©2003 Topham Picturepoint; p.44 ©Corbis Sygma; p.47 ©Kristy-Anne Glubish/Design Pics Inc/Alamy; p.48 ©Dynamic Graphics Group/Creatus/ Alamy; p.50 A ©You Sung-Ho/Corbis, B ©NASA/CalTech/Corbis, C ©Johnny Green/PA/Empics; p.52 all ©Reuters, used with kind permission; p.54 ©Digital Focus/Alamy; p.57 1 ©Martin Jones/Corbis, 2 ©First Hydro Company/Dinorwig Power Station, with kind permission, 3 ©John Noble/ Corbis, 4 ©National Botanical Gardens of Wales, with kind permission, 5 ©Centre for Alternative Technology; p.59 top Impression by courtesy of Edison Mission Energy, bottom ©Jack Sullivan/Alamy; p.60 ©Sue Cunningham/Worldwide Picture Library/Alamy; p.61 ©Gilbert Gilkes & Gordon Ltd, used with kind permission; p.64 ©Wikipedia.org; p.67 ©Dave G. Houser/Corbis; p.70 top ©Rich Iwasaki/Stock Connection/Alamy, A ©Royalty Free/Corbis; p.71 A ©Dallas and John Heaton/Free Agents Ltd/Corbis, B ©Richard Bryant/Arcaid/Alamy; p.73 A ©Frank Chmura/ImageState/Alamy, B ©Bob Krist/Corbis, C ©Benjamin Rondel/Corbis, D ©Derek Croucher/ Corbis, E ©ML Sinibaldi/Corbis; p.76 A ©Royalty Free/Corbis, B ©Bruce Burkhardt/Corbis, C ©Patrick Ward/Corbis, D ©Mark Dyball/Alamy, E ©Angelo Hornak/Corbis; p.79 top ©Andersen-Ross/Brand X Pictures/Alamy, A ©George McLeod; p.84 1 ©Apple Mac used with courtesy of Apple, 2 ©Sony UK used with kind permission, 3 ©Sony UK used with kind permission, 4 ©George McLeod, 5 ©George McLeod; p.89 ©Charlie Borland/FogStock/Alamy; p.90 ©Royalty Free/Corbis; p.93 ©Helen King/Corbis; p.94 1 ©John Powell Photographer/Alamy, 2 ©Duomo/Corbis, 3 ©RubberBall/Alamy, 4 ©Janine Wiedel PhotoLibrary/Alamy, 5 ©Ron Chapple/Think Stock/Alamy; p.97 ©Fitbug UK, used with kind permission; p.99 A ©With kind permission York University, B ©Chris Rainier/Corbis, C ©Buzz Pictures/Alamy, D ©Greenpeace, used with kind permission; p.100 ©Doug Steley/Alamy; p.101 A ©Oxfam and used with kind permission, B ©The Arts Council and used with kind permission, C ©The British Council, used with kind permission, D ©Cancer Research, used with kind permission, E ©The National Trust, used with kind permission; p.102 ©Melanie Friend/Photofusion Picture Library/Alamy; p.104 A ©Andrew Drysdale/Rex Features, B ©David Crausby/Alamy, C ©Ashley Cooper/Picimpact/Corbis; p.109 ©Royalty Free/Corbis; p.111 ©Stone/Getty Images; p.113 left ©Nigel Cattlin/Holt Studios International Ltd/Alamy, centre ©Image100/Alamy, right ©Photodisc; p.116 A ©Sherwin Crasto/Reuters/Corbis, B ©Jacqui Hirst/Corbis, C ©John Madere/Corbis; p.119 ©Camera Crew Photography and University of Bradford; p.126 ©Lester Lefkowitz/Corbis; p.129 ©Royalty Free/Corbis; p.130 ©Liam Bailey/Alamy; p.134 ©Doug Steley/Alamy